A SPECTRUM BOOK

Theodore Needleman

MICRO-COMPUTERS FOR ACCOUNTANTS

PRENTICE-HALL, INC.
Englewood Cliffs, New Jersey 07632

Library of Congress Cataloging in Publication Data

Needleman, Theodore.
   Microcomputers for accountants.

  "A Spectrum Book."
  Bibliography: p.
  Includes index.
    1. Accounting—Data processing. 2. Microcomputers.
I. Title.
HF5679.N43 1983   657'.082'54   82-21583
ISBN 0-13-580696-8
ISBN 0-13-580688-7 (pbk.)

This book is available at a special discount when ordered
in bulk quantities. Contact Prentice-Hall, Inc., General
Publishing Division, Special Sales, Englewood Cliffs, N.J. 07632.

Printed in the United States of America

Editorial/production supervision and interior design by Cyndy Lyle Rymer
Manufacturing buyer Cathie Lenard
Cover design by Hal Siegel

Prentice-Hall International, Inc., *London*
Prentice-Hall of Australia Pty. Limited, *Sydney*
Prentice-Hall of Canada Inc., *Toronto*
Prentice-Hall of India Private Limited, *New Dehli*
Prentice-Hall of Japan, Inc., *Tokyo*
Prentice-Hall of Southeast Asia Pte. Ltd., *Singapore*
Whitehall Books Limited, *Wellington, New Zealand*
Editora Prentice-Hall do Brasil Ltda., *Rio de Janeiro*

CONTENTS

PREFACE

Theodore Needleman, *a specialist in the financial applications of microcomputers and a practicing accountant, is president of his own consulting firm and has written numerous articles for microcomputer magazines.*

There is an old Chinese curse that goes, "May you live in interesting times." The times we live in are, certainly, interesting. The field of accounting has, like most disciplines these days, expanded at an incredible rate. Although the types of tasks that accountants perform have increased so, luckily, have the tools that accountants have available.

When the electronic calculator became widely available in the 1960s, accountants were quick to trade in their old mechanical adding machines and gear-driven calculators. Now that small, personal-size computers are becoming common, it is hardly surprising that accountants are lining up to purchase them. With the many brands and differing models of computers and associated software, the choice of what will work best in your practice is sometimes difficult.

This book will not make you a computer expert overnight. It will give you enough of a background to feel comfortable in making your choice, as well as providing a game-plan for getting a personal computer into your office and providing the assistance so many of our small practices can use.

I would like to thank some of the people who made this book possible: Dave Heinemann, my editor at Prentice-Hall, for his assistance and patience; Barry Leibowicz, friend and attorney for his contributions to some of the legal aspects involved in obtaining a computer; John Moss of BPI Systems, Inc. for his insight over the years as to the producer's side of the software game; and, of course, my wife Lynn, without whose encouragement and assistance this book probably never would have been written.

1

THE MICRO REVOLUTION: A NEW APPROACH TO COMPUTING

A SHORT HISTORY LESSON

In the thousands of years since humans first realized that they could express amounts other than "one" or "many," there have been several generations of computation aids. One of the first counting aids came about with the realization that one could keep track of amounts greater than one by using fingers and toes. The next great leap in computational ability took place with the development of formal numbering systems and the idea of positional notation. The concept of the same digit representing different values depending on where it appears (in the ones' column, tens' column, etc.) is something most adults take for granted, but it probably ranks high on the list of humankind's greatest ideas.

Once the idea of positional notation became known, development of calculating aids quickly followed. This early generation of calculating "hardware" includes devices such as counting sticks, Napier's bones, and the abacus.

Further major developments in calculating aids have taken place in relatively recent times. The first mechanical calculators, such as Babage's "analytical engine," could not be invented until the principles of mechanics and gearing had been developed.

In less than 100 years not only have we gone from strictly mechanical devices to sophisticated electronic marvels, but the use that these devices are put to has also changed. No longer are we concerned only with counting numbers; our concern is now to process data of all types. This ability to process large amounts of many types of data has developed along with the development of the stored-program digital computer.

The earliest electronic computers, developed in the 1920s and during World War II, were *analog* devices. These used the way that certain electronic circuits react to changes in voltage or current to model complex real-world (physical) systems. (For example, analog computers were used extensively during World War II to model and solve ballistics problems, such as artillery and bomb trajectories.) Analog computers were (and to a lesser extent still are) used to perform complex mathematical computations such as integration.

During the 1940s a change in direction took place in the development of computers. Rather then using approximate analog quantities to approximate numerical values, development efforts concentrated on the *digital* computer, which uses binary (on–off/yes–no) logic. Using the binary (base 2) numbering system and later the octal (base 8) and hexidecimal (base 16) systems, it was now possible to express exact numerical values. The use of the binary system gave the digital computer one additional capability that brought the equipment far beyond being just a souped-up adding machine. This additional capability was the internal ability to express a logical decision (a yes–no). This capability is greatly used in computers to perform different actions depending on the result of a prior action.

With the development of the capability of the equipment to store not only the numbers being manipulated but also the sequence of operations that are to be performed (called a *program*), the first *stored-program digital computers* came into being.

Since those early electromechanical computers, we have gone through several generations of both hardware and software. The first generation of electronic digital computers used glass vacuum tubes as logic elements. These early computers were huge devices that took up one or more rooms, used enormous amounts of power, and required special air conditioning to deal with the large amounts of heat produced. These vacuum-tube-based machines also tended to be unreliable and usually required a full-time engineering crew just to keep them operating. They also required a good deal of technical training and expertise on the part of their operators. For all of these inconveniences, they represented a tremendous increase in data handling capability over what had been available before.

The second generation of computers came about with the use of *transistors* instead of vacuum tubes and the development of mass storage devices such as tape units (and later magnetic disk units). The advent of transistors greatly reduced both physical size and power requirements. The development of mass storage devices permitted the system to store large amounts of data to be accessed at a later time. These machines, although still requiring a fair amount of technical expertise to use, do not require a full-time engineering staff just to keep them running. They are much faster than their tube-based predecessors and can handle much greater amounts of data.

The business world was quick to see the advantages of *electronic data processing* (EDP), and during the late 1950s and

FIGURE 1-1 A Second Generation (transistor) Computer System: the IBM 1401. Photo courtesy of IBM.

early 1960s business rather than scientific use became the predominant use for computing equipment.

The third generation of EDP equipment, using *integrated circuits* rather than transistors, made even further inroads into the business world. Although second- and third-generation equipment brought the many benefits of computerized data processing to a large number of businesses, they were (and still are) relatively expensive. While a large or mid-size business may be able to rent a computer for $1000 a month or more, or purchase one for $30,000 or more, few smaller businesses could justify that kind of outlay, regardless of the many benefits such a computer might provide.

In 1976, two articles appeared in different electronic hobbyist magazines. *Radio-Electronics* published build-it-yourself

FIGURE 1–2 A Multi-user Minicomputer: the IBM System/34. Photo courtesy of IBM.

plans for the MARK 8 computer using newly developed "computer-on-a-chip" *microprocessor* integrated circuits. This was followed several months later by *Popular Electronics'* construction articles on the Altair 8080. While these early *microcomputers* required a great deal of technical sophistication to assemble, use, and keep working, they provided the basis and breeding ground for our current crop of personal and "small business" computers. The microprocessor-based computer also instigated a shift in the way people use computing power.

The second- and third-generation *mainframes* and *minicomputers* provided an enormous amount of computing and data handling capacity. Access to this capacity was restricted. A centralized approach was (and still is) used. The individual user submitted his "job," which was then put together with other users' jobs and processed by the computer system in batches.

FIGURE 1–3 A Microprocessor-based Computer System: the IBM Personal Computer. Photo courtesy of IBM.

The major concern was to make the best use of limited computer resources. As computers became more powerful, emphasis shifted to their becoming more user-oriented. Techniques such as *time-sharing* (where a user directly accesses the computer through a terminal) and *remote job entry* (RJE) terminals were developed to provide users less restricted access to computing resources. These concepts eventually led to today's distributed data processing where smaller computers in several locations in a company are used to *preprocess* or half-digest data generated at different locations which is then sent to a larger central computer to be processed further. All these developments have come about because of advances in computer *hardware* (the actual equipment) and computer *software* (the instructions which tell the equipment what to do).

As computer power has grown, computer resources have become much more accessible to the user. In addition, the emphasis has shifted to making these resources easily usable. The recent development of computer systems based on the microprocessor ("computer on a chip") has made it possible for a person with no great technical skills to avail himself of the great benefits of electronic data processing.

THE TWENTY-FIVE-CENT COMPUTER TOUR

Every professional discipline, accounting included, has its set of technical terms or buzzwords. While a glossary is included at the end of this book, it is helpful to introduce some concepts at this point. That way, when you start looking at computer literature or visit a computer store, you will at least be familiar with most of the terms thrown at you.

A computer system consists of three basic types of devices (Fig. 1-4), although more elaborate systems may have more than one of these device types At the heart of any computing system is the *central processing unit* (or CPU). This "box" contains the electronic circuitry which directs information (data and instructions) to and from other devices in the system such as the computer's memory and/or input/output devices (more on this in a moment). The CPU also contains

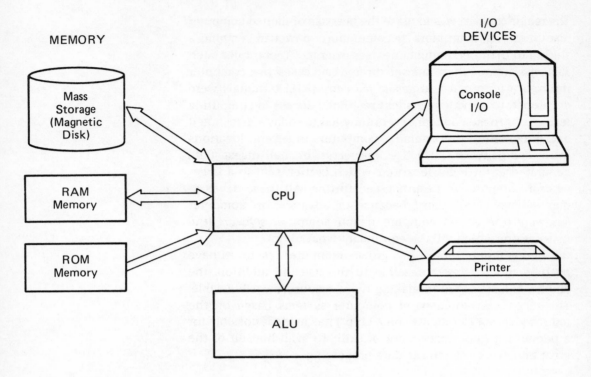

FIGURE 1-4 Computer Organization and Flow

something called the *arithmetic/logical unit* (ALU). This is the electronic circuitry that performs the mathematical operations and, under control of the computer's *program* (list of instructions), makes logical (yes–no) decisions. The actual electronics for both the CPU and ALU may be contained on the same tiny microchip (they usually are in computers of the size we will be concentrating on).

The second basic type of computer device is the computer's memories. There are three basic types of memory in a computer which are used to store (remember) three different types of information. These are *read-only memory* (ROM), *random-access memory* (RAM), and *external mass storage*.

Read-only memory is memory in which information has been entered by the manufacturer before the equipment gets to the user. The computer can read this information but cannot put new information in this area of its memory or change what is there. This type of memory is used for information that, by its nature, does not change, such as a programming language or the computer's operating system (more on this later).

Concerning random-access memory, the computer can both read the information there and also change or write new information into this area (this type of memory is also sometimes called read/write memory). This area of memory is organized into many separate locations each capable of containing one character (which can be a number, letter, or symbol) of information, a byte (Fig. 1-5). This type of memory is called random-access because the computer can go to any one location in this area of memory to read or write a character there, without having to go through all the memory locations preceding it.

Both ROM and RAM are usually contained in the same enclosure (box) as the CPU. While RAM is both easily accessible by the computer and can be read and written to with great speed, it is usually of limited capacity. A small computer system of the type we are discussing generally has internal RAM that can hold between 32,000 and 256,000 characters. This may seem to be quite large, but many data files (payroll records, general ledgers, etc.) can contain many more individual numbers and letters than the computer can hold in its RAM.

External mass storage gets around this limitation. The

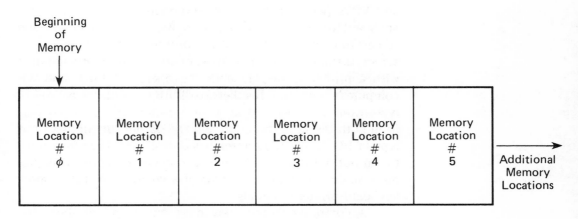

Each Location in Memory Can Store a Character such as
a Letter, Number, or Special Symbol, and is Called a "Byte."

FIGURE 1-5 Memory Organization

most common mass storage devices are *magnetic disk drives* (although earlier personal computers usually used tape cassettes similar or identical to the ones you use with your stereo). There are several types of disk units, and these will be discussed in a later chapter. These disks use a magnetic coating on plastic or metal (similar to a flat, round cassette tape) to store data and programs, and have capacities which range from 100,000 to 80,000,000 characters per unit.

When the computer needs to access data on the disk, it reads data from the disk, stores this data in its fast RAM memory, uses the data if needed, and is able to write the same, or different data back onto the disk. The data stored on the disk takes much longer for the computer to access than data stored in RAM, but the process is still a very rapid one.

The third basic type of computer device, and the last one we will examine, is called an input/output (I/O) device. Before a computer can process data or run a program, the data and/or program must find their way onto the system. After being processed, information must then be presented to human beings. To do this we have input/output devices. Data are input to the computer, processed, and then output to the user. The most common I/O devices used with small computer systems are CRT terminals, printers, and printer/keyboards.

CRT (cathode-ray tube) terminals, sometimes called VDUs and VDTs (video display units/terminals), are made up of a keyboard (to type characters into the system) and a video screen to display both input and output. Instead of the video screen, a similar unit may consist of a keyboard unit combined with a printer to display both the operator's input and the computer's output. This keyboard/printer unit resembles a typewriter. The CRT and keyboard/printer terminal each perform both the input function and the output function. A third type of I/O device, the printer, has only one of these functions, to output information from the computer. Being a single-purpose device, it usually prints at a greater speed than most keyboard/printer terminals.

A computer system may have any or all of these I/O devices attached, but will usually have at least one of these devices capable of both functions (input and output) to be used as the "console I/O device." The console I/O device is used for several functions. It is used not only for data entry and display but also for the operator to select which programs to run.

There are many other devices that can be attached to your computer. These include communications equipment, called *modems*, so that your system can talk to other computers, and even voice I/O devices so that your computer can talk (and listen) to you.

OF BITS, BYTES, AND A FEW OTHER TERMS

Before we proceed, there is just a little more background to cover. All digital computer systems make internal use of some variant of binary (base 2) arithmetic. These internal numbering systems include octal (base 8), hexidecimal (base 16) and BCD (binary-coded decimal). The reason for computer systems using a binary-based numbering system instead of the more familiar decimal (base 10) system is that binary systems are only capable of two states of existence. They are either on or off (think of a light bulb). As the binary numbering system consists of only two digits (zeros and ones), it works very well with digital logic.

The smallest unit of a computers' internal memory is called a *bit*. It is capable of storing only one of two pieces of information, either a one or a zero. Eight of these bits make up one *byte*. A byte is the smallest unit of the computer's memory that can contain one character (a letter, number, or special character) of information.

By use of positional notation, the 8 bits making up a byte can represent any one of 256 different characters (2 to the eighth power, or 2^8 equals 256), although the character set used by most computers (the 26 letters A through Z, 10 digits 0 through 9, and other characters such as the period and comma) is much smaller. A computer's memory capacity is usually given in terms of bytes. Most often this is expressed in K or kilobytes. Although the prefix *kilo* means 1000, because a computer uses binary arithmetic internally, a kilobyte (K) is actually equal to 1024 bytes (or characters of information).

One additional term you may run across fairly frequently is *baud*. This term is used as a measure of serial information transfer speed. The Baud rate is equivalent to the number of bits-per-second transmitted over a serial data line. As mentioned earlier in this chapter, each character of data (a byte) is stored in the computer's memory as a series of bits (each bit is *either* a one *or* a zero). In *serial* data transmission (where each bit is transmitted one after another) several additional bits are added to the data stream to indicate to the receiving computer (or terminal) the start and end of each character. A communications device operating at 300 baud is transmitting and/or receiving information at a speed of about 30 characters per second.

A FEW LAST PIECES OF TERMINOLOGY

Computer literature makes frequent reference to the terms *hardware* and *software*. We have already examined hardware, the physical electronic equipment that makes up a computer system. The other important component of a computer system is its software. Computers have no intelligence per se. They have to be told where information is located and what to do with it. This is accomplished through use of a computer program, which is a detailed set of instructions. There are two general classes of computer software: applications software and system software.

Applications software consists of programs that tell a computer how to do specific tasks, such as general ledger and payroll. *Systems software* consists of programs such as the computer's operating system (which allows the human operator to communicate with the computer) and the computer's languages (such as BASIC). Human beings communicate with other humans (and in their own internal thoughts) in a variety of human languages such as English, French, and Spanish. Computers communicate and internally process in a machine language made up of the two characters zero and one. In order for humans to be able to instruct (or program) the computer, there must be a translation of the instructions (such as "add these two numbers together") into the machine's own binary language of zeros and ones. This is done by means of a computer language. *Computer languages*, such as BASIC, take computer instructions in human-understandable form (these are called programs) and translate them into a binary form the computer can recognize.

Many computer languages have been developed over the years, and each has both advantages and disadvantages. Languages and the forms they come in (compilers, interpreters, and assemblers) will be further discussed in a later chapter.

The terms *microcomputer, minicomputer,* and *mainframe* refer to a computer's size and power. While it used to be quite simple to differentiate between different classes of computers, the demarcation has become less certain in recent times. Microcomputers, sometimes called *personal* or *small-business computers*, generally have the central processing unit (CPU) on one integrated circuit chip. They may be single- or multi-user systems and often equal the more conventional minicomputers in terms of resources available to the user (although usually nowhere near as expensive).

Minicomputers are larger and more expensive than micros. Some of them (*superminis*) can support over 100 users in a time-sharing mode and can cost hundreds of thousands of dollars. Mainframe computers are also expensive and can easily consist of a room full of equipment. In the future, as the power of equipment becomes greater and the physical size and expense of the equipment continues to shrink, we can expect the terms *mini, micro,* and *mainframe* to have progressively less significance.

The systems we will be discussing in this book are considered microcomputers. They are "micro" only in terms of physical size and cost. In terms of computing power and resources, they are the equal of and sometimes superior to machines of a decade ago costing $100,000 or more.

2

WHAT CAN A MICROCOMPUTER DO FOR MY PRACTICE?

An accounting practice has many things in common with any other small business. While accountants render a vital service to the public, a major business objective of an accounting firm, whether large or small, is to render a profit for the firm and provide a living for its employees. A firm must do this while also providing a high level of professional services to its clients.

In larger firms, there is usually a managing partner or managing executive whose job it is to take care of the day-to-day problems of running the business. While an accountant is often consulted by his clients regarding the running of the clients' business, it is common in many smaller practices to find a great deal of neglect in the area of practice management. This is not because the owners don't care about the practice, but they must allocate scarce resources in the most efficient way they can. In most small practices, the scarcest resource is the time available to the accountant and his staff.

Additionally, the paperwork entailed in running a business becomes more and more voluminous every day. There are government reports and tax returns, bookkeeping, and purchasing functions which, as in any other business, take up valuable time. And as in any other business, cash flow must be monitored. Time must be recorded and billed, and receivables must be collected and applied to the clients' accounts. Furthermore, there are reports, letters, statements, and memos to be typed. All of these necessary tasks require staff time, which could be spent more profitably on client work.

On top of these more or less standard business problems, the smaller firm faces increased competition from not only similarly sized firms, but also from larger accounting firms and nonaccounting firms such as bookkeeping and tax services. An additional problem, common to many small practices, arises when staff is currently working at its full capacity. Without additional staff, it becomes impossible to take on new clients. An increase in professional staff usually means a corresponding increase in support staff. Many times this increase in operating costs is greater than the increased revenues expected from an additional client or two.

It is a common saying in the business world that for a business to survive, it must grow. There are several ways that the smaller accounting firm can generate increased cash flow. The most obvious method is to obtain additional clients. More clients will, hopefully, mean more billings. More billings will, hopefully, mean more profits. A second method is to generate additional billings from your current clients. This entails offering (and selling) the client services that your firm does not currently provide. A third, and perhaps less obvious, way is to operate your practice more efficiently, making better use of the people and skills already in the firm.

Large accounting firms have been aware of the benefits of in-house data processing for many years. Microcomputer-based data processing systems can offer the same benefits to the smaller practices. These systems provide an economical solution to many business problems. Besides allowing you to expand your business base by taking on additional clients and offering new services, they also allow you to run the business of your practice more efficiently.

HOW IS ONE OF THOSE
LITTLE BOXES GOING TO DO ALL THAT?

As mentioned before, all computers have similar methods of handling information. While computers can, and do, differ considerably in size, complexity, and expense, given the correct software, a computer that sits on your desk can do the same kinds of data processing that a room sized multi-million dollar system can. A desk-sized micro can do general ledger, process payrolls, and send out bills. The major difference between microcomputers and their larger relatives is capacity, not capability. A large computer may be able to handle a twenty company general ledger consisting of tens of thousands of accounts, while your desktop micro might be limited to processing a company with five or ten divisions comprising five or six hundred accounts. (Many software packages now permit 100 divisions and upwards of 5000 accounts. Peachtree and Datawrite from A.M.I. are two that have extended capacities.)

The mainstay of many small practices consists of client write-up work. Automating client write-up by putting your clients' general ledgers on an in-house microcomputer offers several benefits to both the firm and the client. Computer-based general ledgers are not only faster than doing it by hand, but, in many cases, more accurate. The computer reduces the number of mispostings and the adjusting entries needed to correct them. The reduction in time needed to service your existing clients allows your present staff to service new clients. Processing client data on your own computer allows a faster turnaround and provides your client with more timely financial data. Additionally, financial statements produced as part of the computerized write-up process may provide an opportunity for additional billings if the client does not usually receive them, or reduced typing for your secretary if he does.

Implementing other areas of practice management such as accounts payable and time-and-billing provides up-to-the-minute data on cash flow and better control of receivables. (Few clients send a check without receiving a bill.) Many smaller firms find it impractical to bill their clients on a "time-spent" basis because of the extensive recordkeeping required. Computer-based time-and-billing packages cut down considerably on the amount of effort needed to implement this billing method. There are several benefits to both the firm and the client. The firm may not only be able to bill out previously unbilled work, but reports produced by most computerized time-and-billing software provide the firm with information regarding what kinds of work, and how much, are being done for the client. This may provide an indication of a problem in the client's business operation (if one exists), or with your staff (why is Joe taking six days on a client that should take two?).

Billing on a time-spent basis has some advantages for your clients also. Many times a client has no real knowledge of or appreciation for the amount of time or services provided for him by your firm. A printout of this is very useful in fee negotiations, even with a fixed-fee client.

Practice management also requires control of cash outflows. Implementing a computerized accounts payable package can considerably reduce the amount of time spent on this function as well as provide information needed to make better use of your cash. Many purchases made offer discount terms if paid within a certain time. Most firms do not have the time necessary to do the recordkeeping needed to take advantage of these discounts. On the other side of the coin, many bills get paid before they have to be. Automating the accounts payable process allows you to take discounts where practical and have the use of your cash for the longest period of time possible.

An additional area of practice management where personal computers provide great assistance are the word processing functions which take place in any accounting firm. These time-consuming typing tasks range from once-a-year special reports to report or compilation letters and instructions to your clients. Software is available for most personal computers which turn them into full-function word processors.

Many of these software packages provide features found only on the most expensive, single-purpose word processors, such as the ability to check not only for spelling errors, but also for proper grammar. The ability to generate form letters may seem useless to you at first glance, but its utility becomes obvious when you consider sending a personal letter to each of 50 clients thanking them for their business and wishing them a happy New Year.

This capability is also useful in generating a personal letter to each client to inform him of a tax law change that might affect him. While "personalized" form letters may seem to be a trite way to use a computer, the impression they produce on your client is not.

Every client wants to believe that he is always foremost in the thoughts of his accountant. Practice aids like the above keep clients happy. Couple these with the improved client services a personal computer allows you to provide your client and the result could very possibly be greater client referrals.

Practice management, however, is not the only area personal computers can benefit your practice. Write-up work, discussed before, is one mainstay of the smaller firm. Another service which comprises much of the small practitioner's work is the preparation of tax returns. Many small practices have been convinced of the benefits of processing tax returns with a computer service bureau. These benefits include reduced time to prepare a return and greater accuracy. Preparing tax returns in-house on a personal computer provides these benefits and several others. While using a service bureau to process your returns beats doing them by hand, there are also two major disadvantages. Service bureaus are expensive. Each return may cost from $10 to $20 or more. Tax preparation software, when amortized over the number of returns prepared, is very inexpensive. Even when you add in the expense of a typist (to enter the information into the computer) it is still inexpensive. The second major advantage an in-house computer offers over service bureaus is turnaround. With a service bureau you fill out an input form, send it off, and wait a week or more to see the results. If you (or they) have made an error, an additional week or so is needed. If the mistake was yours, a reprocessing charge is usually charged.

With your own system the turnaround is drastically reduced. While you would generally want to run your returns a batch at a time (possibly overnight), you do have the capability, if needed, to run a tax return while a client is waiting. A mistake made during input means only an additional day's wait, not another week. Additionally, there are many programs available which will allow you to do tax modeling. This enables you to try many different approaches to choose the best strategy for a particular client before you process his return.

Several of the software packages on the market for personal computers are designed specifically for the accountant. These allow the information from a client's general ledger write-up to be fed directly into the tax return preparation program, thus eliminating additional data entry. Software updates for these tax packages are usually available at a fraction of the original purchase price. These updates, issued yearly, reflect changes in tax laws and rates, thus preventing your software from becoming obsolete. An additional feature found in most tax preparation software is the ability to use information for a client entered in a prior year. This frees you from having to re-input information that does not change from year to year such as names, addresses, Social Security numbers, and prior years' incomes used for income averaging.

Another software package that many accountants have found very useful is the "electronic spreadsheet." The first and most famous program of this type is VisiCalc, though there are many similar products now on the market. These spreadsheet programs allow you to build a worksheet of rows and columns on the CRT of your computer. Their most useful feature, however, is that you can define mathematical relationships between different areas on the "sheet." For example, you can define one particular position on the sheet to be equal to the sum of the figures in the column above it. Or you might define a column of numbers to be equal to the column to its left plus 10%. The "magic" of these spreadsheets is that when you change one number, there is also a change in every number on the sheet that has had a relationship defined with the number you change. This feature makes this type of software perfect to use for modeling, forecasting, and budgeting.

"What if" questions ("What if my sales increase 10% every year, while certain expenses decrease 5%" ... etc.) can easily be set up and answered by slotting several different figures in the right place. Many computer dealers claim to have sold entire computer systems on the basis of this one program alone.

The use of off-the-shelf software packages such as Visi-Calc allows the small practitioner to offer his clients many services formerly offered only by much larger firms. Besides being able to easily do pro formas, forecasting, modeling, and budgeting, the smaller firm may also add the capability (at a reasonable cost) of offering clients data processing services such as payroll and other standard applications.

This chapter describes some of the ways personal computers are being used in small practices. There are many other uses, some covered in greater detail in future chapters, that you will find helpful in your practice. Personal computers can be used to access information resources and provide you with 10Ks filed with the SEC, stock prices, and histories from Dow

Jones, and financial information from Dun & Bradstreet. If you do a lot of audit work, you can use your computer to select the sample and analyze the results or to access to the American Institute of Certified Public Accountants (AICPA) time-sharing library. Data base managers and program generators can be used to quickly implement one-of-a-kind applications.

The personal computer is only a tool, but it is a tool whose uses are limited only by your imagination. The nicest feature about a tool of this kind is that the more you use it, the more uses you find for it.

3

GETTING STARTED

Now that you have some idea of what personal computers are and how they can be used, the next step is to decide whether or not to purchase a system. This decision is approached with a two-stage feasibility/system study. While it may seem a little like "overkill" to approach buying an inexpensive piece of equipment with a "formal" plan, using the feasibility/system study methodology will yield several benefits that are not immediately apparent.

Most personal computers are relatively inexpensive (and becoming even more so every day). You may have spent as much, or more, on a photocopy machine or private telephone system. But neither piece of equipment has the potential impact on your business that a computer does. As an accountant, chances are that you have either heard about or observed some disastrous consequences of a poorly planned conversion from one method of recordkeeping to another. This potential exists in any conversion from a manual to automated recordkeeping system, no matter how large or small the data processing equipment is. A well-planned ("formal") approach will minimize the potential for disasters.

A systematic approach may also uncover some weaknesses in existing systems. After all, even accountants can make an occasional mistake. If weaknesses exist, the time to discover them is before a new system is implemented.

A third benefit is that this formalized approach can be used by you to assist your clients in making the same decisions you will have to make. Having been through the process once, you will be in a much better position to advise your clients.

The first part of this approach, the feasibility study, consists of examining all the alternatives involved in implementing various applications. Much of the information gathered in this phase will be used later on in the system study.

The first step in the feasibility study is to examine your practice with a critical eye and classify the work being done into more-or-less discrete "applications" or "job steps." For example a "write-up" client's work might be divided into three distinct steps, "data gathering," "bookkeeping/general ledger," and "closing and tax return preparation." A "review engagement" might be broken down into the following steps: "data gathering," "prepare financial statements," "apply analytical review procedures to statements," and "issue review report."

Perform this procedure on all work currently done in your practice. At this point try to keep your breakdowns as general as possible. As you analyze each job into job steps, make up an informal list such as the one shown in Fig. 3-1. When you have

FIGURE 3-1 Preliminary List of Job Steps

WRITE-UPS

1. Gather Data
2. Bookkeeping/General Ledger
3. Year-end Closing and Tax Return Preparation

REVIEW ENGAGEMENT

1. Gather Data
2. Prepare Financial Statements
3. Apply Analytical Review Procedures
4. Issue Review Report

listed and analyzed services you currently offer to your clients, do the same for services you think you might want to offer. For example, you might want to offer your clients a budgeting report. The job steps for a simple budget variance report might be "list budgeted amounts," "list actual amounts," "compute variances," and "analyze variances and prepare a report."

Once you have analyzed current and future services (don't forget to include services performed internally for the sake of the practice, such as staff evaluation and reports, analysis of expenses and income, etc.) make up a five-column worksheet as shown in Fig. 3-2 (or use the blank form included in the Appendix).

Transfer each application and its associated job steps to the worksheet (use pencil, for you probably will be making a lot of corrections and changes). As you transfer each job step enter in the "Performed by" column the job function level at which the job is performed. Some suggested job level titles are: clerical staff, bookkeeping staff, accounting staff, and principal. Use the job level of the person who actually performs the job (or would perform the job if your firm offered a new service). If your firm consists of just yourself (with not even a clerk or secretary), then use "principal" for each job step. Leave plenty of room between the job steps as you list them.

JOB AND JOB STEP	PERFORMED BY	COST/HOUR	ALTERNATIVES	COST
WRITE-UP:				
Gather Data	Clerical Staff			
Bookkeeping and Posting Client's G/Ls	Bookkeeping Staff			
Analyze G/Ls and Make Up Adjusting Entries	Accounting Staff			
Make Up Year-end Adjustments	Accounting Staff			
Post and Close Books	Bookkeeping Staff			
Prepare Tax Returns and Financial Statements	Accounting Staff			
Type Financial Statements and Tax Returns	Clerical Staff			

FIGURE 3-2 Feasibility Study Worksheet: Step 1

As you transfer each job step to the worksheet, analyze it a bit further. Does the particular job step actually involve several job levels? In our write-up example, the data gathering step gets transferred to the worksheet as is. In transferring the bookkeeping/general ledger (G/L) step we might determine that this actually involves two levels of personnel: a bookkeeper who writes up the client's receipts and disbursements and posts these and adjustments to the general ledger, and an accountant who makes up adjusting entries which are given to the book-keeping staff to post. Because we have determined that this job step actually involves more than one job level, we would transfer it to the worksheet as two job steps: "bookkeeping and posting client's general ledgers" and "analyze general ledgers and make up adjusting entries." In transferring the third write-up step to our worksheet, we might determine that this job step also consists of jobs on different levels.

Closing adjustments might be made up by an accountant, then given to a bookkeeper to post. The accountant might then go into the adjusted books and make up the tax returns and financial statements which are then given to the clerical staff to be typed. (This sequence is shown in Fig. 3-2.) So far, we have made up two separate lists, each analyzing a different function. In our first list, we have taken the "jobs" that are performed in your firm and analyzed them to determine their component "job steps." In making up our second list (the worksheet) we have further analyzed each job step to determine what level of staff performs it. This part of the analysis points out areas where your staff may be doing tasks that can be done by someone less expensive. It is important to be brutally honest in making this analysis. As you fill in the "Performed by" column make sure you note who *is* doing the work, not who *should* be.

Once you have analyzed and transferred all of the jobs on your preliminary list onto the worksheet, you may start the next step in the analysis. Step 2 consists of approximating an hourly cost for each staff level and entering that hourly cost on the worksheet. In the example shown in Fig. 3-3, I have estimated that, on the average, clerical staff costs $5.00 per hour ($200.00 per week divided by 40 hours), bookkeeping staff $7.50 per hour ($300.00 per week divided by 40 hours), and accounting staff

JOB AND JOB STEP	PERFORMED BY	COST/HOUR	ALTERNATIVES	COST
WRITE-UP:				
Gather Data	Clerical Staff	$ 5.00		
Bookkeeping and Posting Client's G/Ls	Bookkeeping Staff	$ 7.50		
Analyze G/Ls and Make Up Adjusting Entries	Accounting Staff	$10.00		
Make Up Year-end Adjustments	Accounting Staff	$10.00		
Post and Close Books	Bookkeeping Staff	$ 7.50		
Prepare Tax Returns and Financial Statements	Accounting Staff	$10.00		
Type Financial Statements and Tax Returns	Clerical Staff	$ 5.00		

ASSUMPTIONS ARE:

Clerical Staff @ $ 5.00/hour ($200/week ÷ 40 hours)
Bookkeeping @ $ 7.50/hour ($300/week ÷ 40 hours)
Accounting @ $10.00/hour ($400/week ÷ 40 hours)

FIGURE 3-3 Feasibility Study Worksheet: Step 2

$10.00 per hour ($400.00 per week divided by 40 hours). Use rates that you feel are realistic. When you have derived hourly rates, fill in this column on the worksheet. This information is used later in the cost-benefit analysis.

Step 3 in our feasibility study consists of examining the individual job steps and determining the alternative ways and costs of doing each. Please note that there may not be alternative ways of accomplishing a job step. Additionally, it may be impossible for you to estimate the cost of an alternative (this is the case with several alternatives in Fig. 3-4). Don't worry about this. The function of this worksheet is to consolidate whatever information we can derive or estimate and to show where there are gaps in our knowledge.

In listing alternatives, restrict yourself to those which will be of some benefit to your firm. As an example, in our analysis of a write-up job a possible alternative to having one of your staff pick up client data (or having client mail it to you) would

JOB AND JOB STEP	PERFORMED BY	COST/HOUR	ALTERNATIVES	COST
WRITE-UP:				
Gather Data	Clerical Staff	$ 5.00	Have Client Key Data Into Our System	Additional Equipment and Phone Lines
Bookkeeping and Posting Client's G/Ls	Bookkeeping Staff	$ 7.50	1) Use Service Bur. 2) In-House D.P. 3) Bookkeeping Svc.	1) $20/month per client 2) Unknown 3) $15/hour
Analyze G/Ls and Make Up Adjusting Entries	Accounting Staff	$10.00	—	—
Make Up Year-end Adjustments	Accounting Staff	$10.00	—	—
Post and Close Books	Bookkeeping Staff	$ 7.50	1) Service Bur. 2) In-House D.P.	1) $15/client 2) Unknown
Prepare Tax Returns and Financial Statements	Accounting Staff	$10.00	1) Service Bur. 2) In-House D.P.	1) $25/client 2) Unknown
Type Financial Statements and Tax Returns	Clerical Staff	$ 5.00	1) In-House D.P. Used for W.P. 2) Typing Service	1) Unknown 2) $10/hour

FIGURE 3-4 Feasibility Study Worksheet: Step 3

be to put a terminal in the client's office and let her tie into your system over the phone (or in your office) and enter her own data. This may or may not be a realistic alternative depending on many factors (the client, the makeup of your practice, the inconvenience and expense of getting the client's data, etc.). If you determine that this might be a realistic alternative, then you should also determine how this alternative would benefit your firm. In this example, the benefits might be decreased workload on your staff, faster turnaround of information to the client, and improved image of your firm to a client.

In listing alternatives try to estimate the cost in dollars per hour if possible. If you are unable to approximate an hourly cost enter the cost in any terms you can approximate. Some alternatives are impossible to estimate (for example, at this point in our study we don't have any idea of what it will cost to purchase an in-house computer). For the present list these costs as "unknown." We will return to these items at a later time when we have more information.

After you have listed alternative methods and their associated costs (wherever possible) for all of your job steps, a qualitative decision must be made. Examine your worksheet. Are there many job steps where data processing will provide a benefit? Are there job steps that you already have computerized with a service bureau that would benefit by being done on the firm's own computer? While there is no practical quantitative method usable at this stage of the study, an examination of the worksheet should at least provide some indication as to whether or not an in-house personal computer is feasible.

Reexamine the worksheet an additional time with an eye to the "reasonableness" of your estimations. Are you being overly optimistic or pessimistic in your estimations? If you added additional applications would your impression of the feasibility change? Would dropping applications change your impressions?

The preliminary worksheet you have just constructed is a handy tool. By constructing it you have not only focused your mind on the specific applications where a personal computer would benefit your practice, but have also provided a foundation for two additional analyses, a cost/benefit analysis and a system study.

The cost/benefit analysis is a familiar technique to all of us. While we cannot yet reasonably estimate costs, we can start listing expected benefits arising from an in-house personal computer. A sample cost/benefit worksheet is illustrated in Fig. 3–5 (a blank worksheet form is included in the Appendix for your convenience).

At this point, list any and all benefits you can think of, whether or not you feel that they are reasonable. Later on, when we are able to start assigning costs, the expected cost will indicate whether an expected benefit is reasonable or not. When you have listed everything you can think of, go back to the previous two lists to see if you have forgotten anything.

The next step in the definition of our wants and needs is the system study. This consists of listing all the applications we wish to implement. This list of applications is derived from examination of the prior worksheets that you have made. If, during the generation of the system study worksheet, you

BENEFITS	COSTS
PRACTICE MANAGEMENT:	
Better Control of Cash Flow	
Word Processing	
Increase Productivity of Current Staff	
In-House Preparation of Tax Returns	
Faster Turnaround than Service Bureau	
CLIENT SUPPORT:	
Faster Turnaround of Information to Client	
More Accuracy in Client Records	
NEW SERVICES:	
Payroll for Clients	
A/R–A/P for Clients	
Budgeting	
Monthly/Quarterly Financial Statements for Clients not Currently Receiving Them	
OTHER BENEFITS:	
Gain Experience for MAS Engagements	

FIGURE 3-5 Preliminary Cost/Benefit Analysis Worksheet

happen to have further thoughts about one of the prior work-sheets, you should add (or change) that particular worksheet. The purpose of these worksheets is to organize information for your use. They are not meant to be either static or works of art, but flexible tools you will use to assist you.

After this is done, examine the list and rank the applications in order of importance. If we could implement only one application, which would it be? What if we could implement two, three, or all of them? A sample worksheet for the system study is illustrated in Fig. 3-6 (a blank worksheet is included in the Appendix).

The ranking of applications is a purely subjective operation and will probably be changed somewhat when you are better able to judge what the cost is in money, time, and effort to implement each application. An excellent starting point for the initial ranking is the benefits part of the cost/benefit worksheet you have started to construct.

Once you have finished the initial ranking, go back to the list and put an asterisk to the left of any application you feel you must have. These should be the applications that you feel

APPLICATION	RELATIVE IMPORTANCE	REQUIRED CAPACITIES	
		NOW	FUTURE (4 YEARS)
•General Ledger (Write-Up)	1	30 Clients 350 Accounts/Client 15 Departments	100 Clients 350 Accounts/Client 25 Departments
• Tax Return Preparation	3	100 Returns/Year Federal/State/City (1040, 1120, 1065)	300 Returns/Year Federal/State/City (1040, 1120, 1065)
• Billing (Accounts Receivable)	2	150 Clients (includes Tax Clients)	400 Clients (includes Tax Clients)
Professional Time Accounting	8	5 Employees	20 Employees
Accounts Payable	6	75 Vendors 100 Checks/Month	150 Vendors 300 Checks/Month
Word Processing	4	10 Letters/Week	30 Letters/Week
NEW CLIENT SERVICES:			
Payroll	7	5 Payrolls/Week 40 Employees/Payroll	15 Payrolls/Week 65 Employees/Payroll
Tax Modeling	5	25 Clients/Year	100 Clients/Year
Budgeting	9	18 Months 300 Accounts 20 Departments	36 Months 300 Accounts 20 Departments
Forecasting	11	24 Periods 200 Accounts	24 Periods 200 Accounts
A/R–A/P	10	5 Clients 100 Customers 100 Vendors 150 Checks/Month	10 Clients 150 Customers 150 Vendors 300 Checks/Month

FIGURE 3-6 System Study Worksheet Example

so strongly about that if they were unavailable, you would not even consider buying a computer. In the example in Fig. 3-6 these applications are general ledger write-up, tax return preparation, and billing (accounts receivable). Note that in the example, these applications are ranked from number 1 to number 3. A gap in the ranking (for example, if the three "must have" applications had rankings of 1, 2, and 5) would indicate that either the relative importance had been misstated or that you have forgotten to asterisk a "must have" application.

When you are satisfied with the ranking (at least for the moment), proceed to the most difficult part of the system study, estimating required capacities. Estimating capacities is a difficult task because it requires not only that you be brutally honest with yourself and that you have a touch of the fortune teller in you, but also that you compensate for your own natural optimism (or pessimism, if that be the case). Overestimate your requirements and you wind up with a machine which will always be underutilized. Underestimate, and you wind up limited in what you can accomplish with the system. While most personal computers are expandable into fairly large systems, some are more easily expandable than others. Choosing the right-size system for both current and reasonable future needs will save you time, money, and aggravation down the road.

One additional idea to keep in mind in estimating capacities is that when in doubt, it is better to overestimate your needs than to underestimate them. You can always underutilize a machine with excess capacity, but you can't overutilize a machine with limited capacity.

Take your system study worksheet and, for each application, estimate the capacities needed now. Express these capacities in terms of the application. This is because different software and hardware products use the computer's resources differently. For example, one supplier's general ledger software may require 250,000 characters of disk storage to hold a client ledger with 200 accounts in it, while a different supplier's software might require more or less storage to hold the same client information. In estimating our currently required capacity for general ledger write-up we would first examine the largest write-up client currently served by the practice. How large a chart of accounts does the client have? Is there a need to report by departments? (In most general ledger software, departmentalizing also allows you to consolidate multicompany clients.)

In analyzing this client we find that he currently has 12 departments and a total of 300 accounts counting each departmental account as a separate account (i.e., cash in bank–Department 1 and cash in bank–Department 2 are two separate accounts). Adding some additional capacity for current year growth, we estimate that our current need in a general ledger write-up system is the capacity to handle a client with 15 departments and 350 accounts in its chart of accounts. We also estimate that we will, in the current year, want to put 30 of our client's write-ups on the computer. These required current capacities are reflected in the sample worksheet illustrated in Fig. 3-6.

The next application in our example is tax return preparation. (In making your estimates work from the top down rather than in order of relative importance. This is easier than skipping all over the page.) In this application we estimate that we currently process 100 returns per year. These returns consist, for the most part, of federal, state, and possibly local or city returns for each client and encompass forms 1040, 1120, and 1065.

Continue down the worksheet, filling in your best estimates of current requirements. When this is finished, we must do the same for our future requirements. Before we can do this, we must pick a point in time as the "future." This is a totally subjective and individual choice. In the sample worksheet, I have chosen the future to be four years from now. My reasons for using four years rather than two or six are as follows:

1. Less than three years (e.g., two years) is not a very long time from now and does not permit the reasonable projection of much growth without postulating "overnight success."

2. The future beyond five years from now is too difficult to predict.

3. Most equipment in the price range of personal computers has a useful life of three to five years. While computer equipment does not generally "wear out" in this time frame, you can be fairly certain that developments in the field within the next three to five years will precipitate a case of "new model fever" similar to that which strikes many of us when a new car model is introduced. The technology in micros is advancing so rapidly that equipment purchased four years ago is now obsolete.

You are welcome to borrow any or all of the above rationalizations in choosing your "future." Once you have chosen your time frame, go down the list again and estimate, as reasonably as possible, anticipated requirements. You may want to estimate the firm's growth at the same rate as inflation. In making your estimates, don't forget that having a computer will be a factor, and have an effect, in the growth of your firm.

When you finish this column, put the worksheets aside for the moment. We will use them again later as we accumulate more information.

As an example of how the system study worksheet (Fig. 3-6) can be used to calculate required storage capacities, we will make some assumptions about the storage requirements for each application and use these figures to calculate total required storage. Many software producers will be able to supply you with these figures for their packages (if they can't, you will have to estimate).

General Ledger: requires 55 bytes per account, 22 bytes per transaction line (a transaction is any entry into any journal), and 400,000 bytes for storage of programs of which 180,000 bytes must be on line (accessible without changing disks) at one time.

Tax Return Preparation: requires 2,000 bytes per client and 350,000 bytes for program storage (of which 200,000 bytes must be on line at one time).

Billing (Accounts Receivable): requires 200 bytes per client and 400,000 bytes for program storage (100,000 bytes on line at one time). Also requires 50 bytes per invoice line (estimate 5 invoice lines per client).

Professional Time Accounting: 400 bytes per employee, 100 bytes per transaction line, and 500,000 bytes for program storage (of which 230,000 bytes must be on line at one time).

Accounts Payable: 400 bytes for each vendor, 100 bytes per invoice line transaction, 300,000 bytes for program storage (of which 190,000 bytes must be on line at all times).

Word Processing: requires an average of 10,000 bytes for each letter and 100,000 for program storage.

Payroll: requires 250 bytes for each employee master record, 50 bytes per employee per week, and 300,000 bytes for program storage (of which 100,000 bytes must be on line at one time).

Tax Modeling: requires 50,000 bytes per client, 30,000 bytes for program storage.

Budgeting: requires 10 bytes per account, 150,000 bytes for program storage (all on line at one time).

Forecasting: same storage requirements as Budgeting.

Client A/R–A/P: requirements as above.

Note: The figures used here are for illustrative purposes only and are not representative of any particular software. When you make *your* calculations, use figures for the particular brand of software you are considering. *Do not use* above figures in *your* calculations!

Calculations: (calculations are shown first for a hard disk based system, then for a floppy disk based system). All calculations are done in two steps; first data storage requirements are calculated, then program storage requirements are added on.

General Ledger Step 1:
Data Storage Requirements

	NOW	FUTURE
Accounts/client	350	350
Departments	×15	×25
Accounts	5250	8750
Bytes/Account	×55	×55
Bytes	288,750	481,250
Clients	×30	×100
Bytes total storage for Chart of Accounts	8,662,500	48,125,000
Bytes per transaction line	20	20
Transaction lines/ Month	×1500	×1500
Bytes	30,000	30,000
Clients	×30	×100
Bytes Total Storage for 1 Month's Transactions	900,000	3,000,000

General Ledger Step 2:
Add in Program Storage Requirements
Total Storage Requirements for General Ledger

	NOW	FUTURE
Chart of Accounts	8,662,500	48,125,000
Transactions	900,000	3,000,000
Program Storage	400,000	400,000
TOTAL	9,962,500	51,525,000

Tax Return Preparation Step 1

	NOW	FUTURE
Bytes/client	2,000	2,000
Returns	×100	×300
	200,000	600,000

Tax Return Preparation Step 2

	NOW	FUTURE
Data storage	200,000	600,000
Program Storage	350,000	350,000
TOTAL	550,000	950,000

Billing (Accounts Receivable) Step 1

	NOW	FUTURE
Bytes per invoice line	50	50
Invoice lines per statement	×5	×5
Bytes	250	250
Bytes per client	+200	+200
Bytes Data Storage per client	450	450
Clients	×150	×400
TOTAL	67,500	180,000

Billing (Accounts Receivable) Step 2:
Add in Required Program Storage

	NOW	FUTURE
Data Storage	67,500	180,000
Program Storage	400,000	400,000
TOTAL	467,500	580,000

	NOW	FUTURE

Professional Time Accounting Step 1

	NOW	FUTURE
Bytes per employee	400	400
Employees	×5	×20
Bytes Storage for Employee Master Records	2000	8000
Bytes per Transaction Line	100	100
Transaction Lines (2 Transactions/day × 20 days per month)	×40	×40
Bytes per Month per employee	4000	4000
Employees	×5	×20
Bytes Storage for 1 Month's Transactions	20,000	80,000

Professional Time Accounting Step 2:
Add in Requirements for Program Storage

	NOW	FUTURE
Storage for Employee Master Records	2,000	8,000
Storage for 1 Month's Transactions	20,000	80,000
Program Storage	500,000	500,000
TOTAL	522,000	588,000

Accounts Payable Step 1

	NOW	FUTURE
Bytes per vendor	400	400
Bytes	×75	×150
Storage for Vendor Master Records	30,000	60,000
Bytes per Transaction Line	100	100
Transaction lines per check (estimated)	×2	×2
	200	200
Checks per Month	×100	×300
Bytes for 1 Month's Transactions	20,000	60,000

Accounts Payable Step 2:
Add in Requirements for Program Storage

	NOW	FUTURE
Storage for Vendor Master Records	30,000	60,000
Storage for 1 Month's Transactions	20,000	60,000
Program Storage	300,000	300,000
TOTAL	350,000	420,000

	NOW	FUTURE

Word Processing Step 1

	NOW	FUTURE
Bytes per Letter Document	10,000	10,000
Documents/month (= letters per week × 4.3 weeks per month)	×43	×129
TOTAL	430,000	1,290,000

Word Processing Step 2:
Add in Requirements for Program Storage

	NOW	FUTURE
Document Storage	430,000	1,290,000
Program Storage	100,000	100,000
TOTAL	530,000	1,390,000

Payroll Step 1

	NOW	FUTURE
Bytes per Employee Master Record	250	250
Employees	×40	×65
	10,000	16,250
Payrolls per week	×5	×15
Storage for Employee Master Records	50,000	243,750
Bytes per employee per week	50	50
Employees	×40	×65
	2,000	3,250
Payrolls per week	×5	×15
Storage for Employee Transaction Records	10,000	48,750

Payroll Step 2:
Add in Requirements for Program Storage

	NOW	FUTURE
Storage for Employee Master Records	50,000	243,750
Storage for Employee Transaction Records	10,000	48,750
Program Storage	300,000	300,000
TOTAL	360,000	592,500

Tax Modeling Step 1

	NOW	FUTURE
Bytes per Client	50,000	50,000
Clients	×25	×100
	1,250,000	5,000,000

	NOW	FUTURE

Tax Modeling Step 2:
Add in Requirements for Program Storage

	NOW	FUTURE
Data Storage	1,250,000	5,000,000
Program Storage	30,000	30,000
TOTAL	1,280,000	5,030,000

Budgeting Step 1

	NOW	FUTURE
Bytes per Account	10	10
Accounts	×300	×300
Bytes	3,000	3,000
Departments	×20	×20
Bytes	60,000	60,000
Months	×18	×36
Bytes for Data Storage	1,080,000	2,160,000

Budgeting Step 2:
Add in Requirements for Program Storage

	NOW	FUTURE
Data Storage	1,080,000	2,160,000
Program Storage	150,000	150,000
TOTAL	1,230,000	2,310,000

Forecasting Step 1

	NOW	FUTURE
Bytes per Account	10	10
Accounts	×200	×200
Bytes	2,000	2,000
Periods	×24	×24
Bytes for Data Storage	48,000	48,000

Forecasting Step 2:
Add in Requirements for Program Storage

	NOW	FUTURE
Data Storage	48,000	48,000
Program Storage	150,000	150,000
TOTAL	198,000	198,000

	NOW	FUTURE

A/R–A/P (For Clients) Step 1

	NOW	FUTURE
Bytes per invoice line	50	50
Invoice lines per statement	×5	×5
Bytes per statement	250	250
Statements per client	×100	×100
	25,000	25,000
Number of clients	×5	×10
Data Storage for Client A/R's	125,000	250,000
Bytes per vendor	400	400
Number of Vendors	×100	×150
Storage for Vendor Master Records	40,000	60,000
Bytes per Transaction Line	100	100
Transaction Lines per check	×2	×2
	200	200
Checks per client	×150	×300
	30,000	60,000
Number of clients	×5	×10
Data Storage for A/P Transactions	150,000	600,000

A/R–A/P (For Clients) Step 2:
Add in Requirements for Program Storage

	NOW	FUTURE
Data Storage for Client A/R's	125,000	250,000
Data Storage for Vendor Master Records	40,000	60,000
Data Storage for A/P Transactions	150,000	600,000
Program Storage A/R Programs	400,000	400,000
Program Storage A/P Programs	300,000	300,000
TOTAL	1,015,000	1,610,000

A table summarizing the results of these calculations can be found in Fig. 3–7 (p. 45).

The second series of calculations, those for a floppy disk based system, are made a bit differently. After we have made these calculations, we will examine both sets of results (those for both hard and floppy disk based systems) and demonstrate how the results can help you decide on hardware requirements.

In calculating requirements for floppy based systems we make several additional assumptions:

1. The system will require at least two floppy disk drives, one on which the programs will reside, the second to hold data files.
2. Program storage requirements will be defined as the amount of disk storage required to be on line at one time.
3. Data storage requirements are calculated for *one* client. It is assumed that a separate diskette will be used for each client.

	NOW	FUTURE

General Ledger

	NOW	FUTURE
Accounts/client	350	350
Departments	×15	×25
Accounts	5,250	8,750
Bytes/Account	×55	×55
Bytes	288,750	481,250
Bytes per Transaction Line	20	20
Transaction lines/month	×1500	×1500
Bytes	30,000	30,000
Storage for Chart of Accounts	288,750	481,250
Storage for Transactions	30,000	30,000
Data Storage Required	318,750	511,250

Tax Return Preparation

	NOW	FUTURE
Bytes/client	2,000	2,000
Data Storage Required	2,000	2,000

Billing (Accounts Receivable)

	NOW	FUTURE
Bytes per invoice line	50	50
Invoice lines per statement	×5	×5
Bytes	250	250
Bytes per client	+200	+200
Bytes Data Storage per Client	450	450

	NOW	FUTURE

Professional Time Accounting

	NOW	FUTURE
Bytes per employee	400	400
Employees	×5	×20
Bytes storage for Employee Master Records	2,000	8,000
Bytes per Transaction Line	100	100
Transaction lines	×40	×40
Bytes per month per employee	4,000	4,000
Employees	×5	×20
Bytes storage for 1 month's transactions	20,000	80,000
Data Storage for Employee Master Records	2,000	8,000
Data Storage for Transaction Lines	20,000	80,000
Total Data Storage Required	22,000	88,000

Accounts Payable

	NOW	FUTURE
Bytes per vendor	400	400
Bytes	×75	×150
Storage for vendor Master Records	30,000	60,000
Bytes per Transaction Line	100	100
Transaction lines per check (estimated)	×2	×2
	200	200
Checks per month	×100	×300
Bytes for 1 month's Transactions	20,000	60,000
Storage for Vendor Master Records	30,000	60,000
Storage for 1 month's Transactions	20,000	60,000
Total Data Storage Required	50,000	120,000

Word Processing

	NOW	FUTURE
Bytes per letter document	10,000	10,000
Documents/month	×43	×129
Data Storage Required	430,000	1,290,000

Payroll

	NOW	FUTURE
Bytes per employee	250	250
Employees	×40	×65
Storage for employee Master Records	10,000	16,250

	NOW	FUTURE
Bytes per employee per week	50	50
Number of employees	×40	×65
Storage for employee transaction records	2,000	3,250
Storage required for employee Master Records	10,000	16,250
Storage required for employee transaction records	2,000	3,250
Total Data Storage Required	12,000	19,500

Tax Modeling

	NOW	FUTURE
Bytes per client	50,000	50,000

Budgeting

	NOW	FUTURE
Bytes per account	10	10
Accounts	×300	×300
	3,000	3,000
Departments	×20	×20
	60,000	60,000
Months	×18	×36
Bytes of Data Storage Required	1,080,000	2,160,000

Forecasting

	NOW	FUTURE
Bytes per account	10	10
Accounts	×200	×200
	2,000	2,000
Periods	×24	×24
Bytes of Data Storage Required	48,000	48,000

A/R (For Clients)

	NOW	FUTURE
Bytes per invoice line	50	50
Invoice lines per statement	×5	×5
Bytes per statement	250	250
Statements per client	×100	×100
Data Storage for Client A/R	25,000	25,000

	NOW	FUTURE
Bytes per vendor	4400	400
Number of vendors	×100	×150
Storage for vendor Master Records	40,000	60,000
Bytes per transaction line	100	100
Transaction lines per check	×2	×2
	200	200
Checks per client	×150	×300
Data Storage for A/P Transactions	30,000	60,000
Storage required for vendor Master Records	40,000	60,000
Storage required for A/P Transactions	30,000	60,000
Total Data Storage Required	70,000	120,000

The results of the above calculations are summarized in Fig. 3-8.

FIGURE 3-7 Summary Table: Hard Disk Storage Requirements Example

APPLICATION	DATA STORAGE REQUIRED (NOW) IN BYTES	DATA STORAGE REQUIRED (FUTURE) IN BYTES	PROGRAM STORAGE REQUIRED	ON LINE PROGRAM STORAGE REQUIRED
General Ledger	9,562,500	51,125,000	400,000	180,000
Tax Return Preparation	200,000	600,000	350,000	200,000
Billing (Accounts Receivable)	67,500	180,000	400,000	100,000
Professional Time Accounting	22,000	88,000	500,000	230,000
Accounts Payable	50,000	120,000	300,000	190,000
Word Processing	430,000	1,290,000	100,000	100,000
Payroll	60,000	292,500	300,000	100,000
Tax Modeling	1,250,000	5,000,000	30,000	30,000
Budgeting	1,080,000	2,160,000	150,000	150,000
Forecasting	48,000	48,000	150,000	150,000
A/R–A/P	315,000	910,000	700,000	190,000
TOTALS	13,085,000	61,813,500	3,380,000	1,620,000

APPLICATION	DATA STORAGE REQUIRED NOW (IN BYTES)	DATA STORAGE REQUIRED FUTURE (IN BYTES)	ON LINE PROGRAM STORAGE REQUIRED
General Ledger	318,750	511,250	180,000
Tax Return Preparation	2,000	2,000	200,000
Billing (Accounts Receivable)	450	450	100,000
Professional Time Accounting	22,000	88,000	230,000
Accounts Payable	50,000	120,000	190,000
Word Processing	430,000	1,290,000	100,000
Payroll	12,000	19,500	100,000
Tax Modeling	50,000	50,000	30,000
Budgeting	1,080,000	2,160,000	150,000
Forecasting	48,000	48,000	150,000
A/R (for clients)	25,000	25,000	100,000
A/P (for clients)	70,000	120,000	190,000

FIGURE 3–8 Summary Table: Floppy Disk Storage Requirements Example

EVALUATING THE RESULTS

In examining the summary table in Fig. 3-7 (Hard Disk Storage Requirements) several points are apparent.

1. If all applications are to be implemented to meet our current needs we would need a hard disk with a capacity in excess of 16,465,000 bytes:

Data Storage Required (Now)	13,085,000
Program Storage Required	3,380,000
	16,465,000

   As 20 megabyte (20,000,000) disks are available, this will meet our current requirements.

2. To meet our future needs will require drives with capacity in excess of 65,193,500 bytes:

Data Storage Required (Future)	61,813,500
Program Storage Required	3,380,000
	65,193,500

Analysis

This approach requires that within the next four years (the time period assumed for "future") and assuming no change in "state-of-the-art," we would need to purchase at least three additional hard disk drives (two 20 megabyte and one 10 megabyte). This will entail a large outlay of funds to meet expansion needs. This amount could easily equal or exceed the purchase price for your original system. On first analysis, this does not appear to be an optimum approach. For the moment, we will reserve judgment and examine the results summarized in Fig. 3-8 (Floppy Disk Storage Requirements). Several points in this table are also apparent at first glance.

1. The largest requirement for on line program storage is 230,000 bytes (for Professional Time Accounting).
2. There are 3 applications that have large current storage requirements:

Budgeting	1,080,000 bytes
Word Processing	430,000 bytes
General Ledger	318,750 bytes

3. These same 3 applications also have large future storage requirements:

Budgeting	2,160,000 bytes
Word Processing	1,290,000 bytes
General Ledger	511,250 bytes

Analysis

1. The required capacity of at least 230,000 bytes for the program storage drive should not be a problem. A "standard" 8 inch, single sided, single density flopy disk drive running under the CP/M operating system has a capacity of approximately 250,000 bytes. One of these drives would suffice.

2. The data storage requirements provide a bit of a problem. Using "double-density" (stores about 500,000 bytes per disk), or "quad-density" (stores over 1 megabyte per disk) disk drives will satisfy our

current and projected future needs for data storage for General Ledger. If we examine our original assumptions about word processing applications, we notice that each letter document requires an average of 10,000 bytes. If we store less letters on each word processing data storage disk, eight inch floppy disk drives will easily satisfy our current and future data storage requirements for this application.

3. Budgeting, however, will be a problem. If we cannot construct smaller budget models or find software that uses less disk storage than the software being currently considered, we must make a choice: either abandon implementing this particular application or implement a hard disk system.

While our analysis to this point seems to favor a floppy disk based system, there is one more solution we should examine. We could implement a system that has a combination of hard and floppy disk storage: A 10 megabyte hard disk and a "double-density" (500,000 byte capacity) 8 inch floppy disk. In this configuration, we would keep all of our programs, as well as the data storage for the budgeting application on the hard disk. When we run an application, we would transfer the data stored for a particular client and application from the 8 inch floppy disk *onto* the hard disk. After the application has been run, we would transfer the *updated* data back onto 8 inch floppies and free up the hard disk for the next client and/or application. This approach has several benefits:

1. We get most of the current and future benefits of having a hard disk without the problem of having to add multiple hard disks in the future.
2. This method automatically "backs-up" your files onto the floppy disks ("back-up" is discussed in a later chapter).
3. As all processing takes place with the programs and data residing on the hard disk, the system will run *much* faster than a strictly floppy-based system, especially with larger data files.
4. Because the data storage for the budgeting application is kept on the hard disk, the problems associated in implementing this application on floppy disk based systems do not apply.

This comprehensive example has illustrated some techniques that you will find useful. It has also shown that sometimes going a little beyond the obvious will produce a "better way."

4

CONSULTANTS: PURCHASING KNOWLEDGE AND EXPERIENCE

While many clients tend to view accountants as experts regarding anything having to do with numbers or finance, most accountants tend to concentrate on the particular areas of accounting which they personally find most interesting. They tend to form loose associations with other professionals with expertise in areas other than their own. When one of their clients has a problem outside their realm, they bring in one of these consultants, on a formal or informal basis, to provide additional expertise.

Just as accountants make use of outside expertise to assist their clients, it may make sense to go to an outside consultant for help in getting an in-house personal computer set up and assisting in the practice.

The process of getting a computer up and running can be subdivided into five phases. These phases are the feasibility study, the systems study (both covered in the prior chapter), the research phase, the acquisition phase, and the installation and training phase (covered in succeeding chapters). While a consultant experienced in data processing can be engaged to handle the entire process of obtaining and installing the computer, it may not make sense to use him in this fashion. For a consultant to be of use to you, he must be given a fairly complete background of your business. There is no such thing as a "standard" accounting practice. While your practice probably has much in common with other professional practices, there are still things that you want done "your" way. It is also unreasonable to expect an outsider to know your business as well as you do.

When a consultant is engaged, the first thing he is going to do is to try to obtain a "feel" for what you are doing now and what you wish to do in the future. He will want to know what applications you desire to implement and what current and future capacities will be needed. This is, of course, the information you would collect during the feasibility and system study. Whether you write down the information (as detailed in the preceding chapter) or recite the information to the consultant for him to write down, realize that it is you who will have to provide most of the information needed in the initial phases.

When engaging a consultant on behalf of a client, the accountant does so to provide an extension of her abilities and expertise. In using a consultant on her own behalf, the same yardstick applies. A consultant should be used to provide a backup in areas where the accountant has little or no expertise and cannot readily develop it.

Accountants are, by training and experience, expert in financial information systems and business organization. This expertise, coupled with your intimate knowledge of how your particular practice works, makes you the most qualified person to do feasibility and system studies. If, however, a consultant is engaged, you should request that he review your feasibility and system studies (most consultants will insist on doing this anyway).

There are two reasons for having a consultant review your work, neither of which reflects in any way on your integrity, experience, or intelligence. Many accountants, while expert on the mechanics of financial systems, do not have a clear understanding of how computers are most effectively used in these processes. A consultant, by education, training, and experience, does. Additionally, a consultant, by virtue of being an outsider, may be able to see items in the feasibility and system studies that you have misjudged or forgotten simply because you are "too close" to them.

If, in engaging a consultant, you are purchasing expertise and knowledge, it makes sense to make the best use of this backup capability. Reviewing your feasibility and system studies is one area where a consultant is useful. The phase where you may find a consultant most useful, however, is the research phase. This phase, described in detail in the next chapter, consists of gathering as much information as possible on hardware and software and their relationship to what you wish to do in your practice. This phase is the most time-consuming part of getting a computer working for you. It is also the most important phase. No one—consultants, sales-persons, friends—can tell you which software/hardware com-bination is the best for your use. They can only suggest and recommend. The final decision is yours. The more information you have, the better decision you will be able to make.

Most consultants in the data processing field spend much of their time staying up to date with developments in the field. They are familiar with much (though usually not all) of the hardware and software available. Their experience gives them a good idea of generally what will work in a particular set of cir-cumstances, and, more importantly, what will not. Many disas-ters encountered in the purchase of a computer can be traced back to the purchaser's not obtaining enough information before making the purchase.

Hiring a consultant to assist you will not absolve you from your responsibility to become as knowledgeable as possible on the subject of computers. The consultant can act as a filter in dealing with the enormous amount of information that exists. He can advise you as to the areas in your business where there may be problems. He can, in effect, act as your "legman," gathering much of the information you will need to make your decision. Additionally, a consultant can most likely do this in much less time than you. Most consultants can save steps since they know where to go for specific information.

A consultant can also be helpful in the final three phases of the project: acquisition, installation, and training. A con-sultant who has amassed a fair amount of experience has no doubt had dealings with the computer suppliers in your area. His opinion and experience with other installations can provide a good indication of how responsive a particular dealer will be after the sale is made. Having your "expert" along while talking to salespersons provides you with a quick indication of whether you are listening to double-talk. A consultant's presence during sales discussions also tends to have a stifling effect on another common problem, that of "oversell."

Once a computer has been decided upon and purchased, problems cropping up during and after installation and training are usually handled between you and the supplier. A consultant who has been involved to this point may prove to be a valuable resource in resolving such problems.

We've covered some of the whys, whens, and wheres of using a consultant. The next questions to consider are who to use and how to use him. Finding a knowledgeable, independent consultant is not always an easy task. Anyone can call himself a consultant. While there is a certification program for people working in the data processing field (the Certified Data Processor designation is awarded upon passing a difficult examination and having requisite experience), possession of this certificate is no guarantee that the holder is expert in all phases of data processing any more than the CPA certificate guarantees expertise in all areas of accounting. Making the choice even more difficult, there are many excellent consultants who do not hold the CDP certificate, or even a college degree.

The most likely place to start to look for a consultant is among your peers. Many smaller accounting firms have developed considerable expertise in the data processing field (as you hopefully will). Additionally, your local chapter of the AICPA, state accounting society, or other accounting organizations such as the National Association of Accountants or American Accounting Association, may be able to recommend a consultant. Other places to look for a consultant include the Data Processing Managers Association (DPMA), the Association for Computing Machinery (ACM), and users groups such as the Boston Computer Society (and others). Check local computer stores' bulletin boards for local groups. Another source for consultants may be a local college. Many have faculty members who do outside consulting work.

Suitably armed with the name (or names) of some local expert, the next step is to set up preliminary consultation. You will use these preliminary consultations to answer the following three questions:

1. Do I need a consultant?
2. If I do, in what areas would a consultant be useful?
3. If a consultant would be helpful, why should I choose this one rather than someone else?

These questions will be answered with information gathered during your conversation. This interview should hopefully take the form of a conversation rather than an inquisition. Remember, you are looking for a partner in the enterprise of getting a

FIGURE 4-1 Evaluation Interview Checklist

☐ INDEPENDENCE

☐ EDUCATION

☐ EXPERIENCE

☐ REFERENCES

☐ AVAILABILITY

☐ ATTITUDE

☐ OTHER SERVICES OFFERED

☐ FEE STRUCTURE

computer up and running in your practice. Don't be afraid to ask a direct question if need be. In the final analysis, a consultant's purpose is to help you. There are some areas that you should cover in interviewing a prospective consultant. These areas are listed in Fig. 4-1 (Evaluation Interview Checklist) and discussed in detail below. While I don't recommend that you stride into the consultant's office with the checklist attached to a clipboard and make a production out of checking off each item, covering all the items on the list should provide the answers to the three questions posed above.

In considering the engagement of a consultant, one of the most important areas to cover is the consultant's independent status. A consultant who works for a manufacturer or supplier cannot be relied upon to have your best interest in mind. While it is not unreasonable that a consultant may have contacts with manufacturers and suppliers, it is important that the consultant you choose be open-minded. While it is possible that a particular piece of hardware or software is perfect for 99% of the people who buy it, it does not necessarily follow that it is the best for you. You know this, and a good, independent consultant knows this also.

The other most important thing to look for in a consultant is his ability. This includes his education, experience, and references. While a college degree or certification may provide some reassurance as to a consultant's competence, there is no substitute for experience. Establish that a potential consultant has not only knowledge in the areas you may wish to use him, but also that he has "real-world" experience. Any reputable consultant will provide references if requested. Ask for them. Call the people given as references. What did the consultant do for them? When? What did they like about him? What did they dislike? Would they (did they) use him again? Be suspicious if you call four or five references and never hear one bad word. Remember when something (or someone) sounds "too-good-to-be-true," it usually is.

Another item to cover during this interview is the availability of the consultant. How accessible is he to answer unforeseen questions? In making the appointment for this initial interview, how long did you have to wait? While it is unreasonable to expect a consultant to be at your beck and call 24 hours a day, 7 days a week (like you are to your clients), your fee should assure that your questions will be answered promptly, that you won't have to wait a month for a return phone call.

Also important is the consultant's attitude. Did he snicker when you showed him your initial feasibility study? You have come to the consultant because you know that no one person can be expert in everything. If the consultant you are interviewing knows that he is the one exception to the rule, he is not the right person for the job. You are a professional at what you do and have the right to expect the same attitude from any other professional you choose to work with you. After all, you don't ridicule a client for asking a question you might consider "silly."

Other items you should discuss are the consultant's fee structure and whether services other than advisory are offered. Many consultants charge on a "time-spent" basis, either hourly or daily. Many consulting firms offer additional services besides their "advisory" service. These can include custom programming, modifying packaged software, and software maintenance (fixing any problems that come up in the software). It is a good idea to find out if the consultant you are considering offers these services and, if he does, what he charges for them.

Once you have decided to use a consultant and have one who you think will work well with you, sit down and consider exactly where and how you intend to use his services. Many consultants use either an engagement letter or contract. If the consultant you have chosen is not familiar with this practice, you may want to make up the engagement letter yourself. By no means engage a consultant without some form of written agreement setting forth what is expected and what the charges will be for those services.

Many consultants will insist on the right to purchase documentation on your behalf and either charge you for the purchase or have the purchase billed to you. This is a common practice and is usually beneficial to you. The purchase of a manual usually provides the consultant with much more information on the suitability of a product for your use than he would be able to gain from other sources. You will probably want to specify a dollar limit that the consultant can spend on your behalf beyond which the expenditure would require your written authorization.

If the consultant has supplied an engagement letter or contract, forward a copy to your lawyer. Don't sign anything without knowing exactly what the rights and responsibilities of each of you will be. The purpose of the agreement is to protect both parties.

Using a consultant can save you time, energy, and money. A good consultant can provide an additional area of expertise to your firm. Remember, though, that the main function of any consultant is to advise you. A consultant may recommend a specific purchase or several choices that he feels would best serve your needs. The final decision on whether to buy, and if so, what to buy, is yours.

5

GATHERING INFORMATION AND STARTING TO MAKE DECISIONS

So far we have seen how a personal computer can help in your practice and have started to gather the data needed to choose the correct software and hardware. In this chapter we will detail what additional information is needed, how to go about getting it, and how best to use the information obtained.

The data gathering or research phase is the most time-consuming part of getting a computer up and running in your practice. This is because you must obtain some degree of understanding about computers to be able to analyze the information you gather. While no one expects you to become a computer expert, it is in your own self-interest to have some understanding as to what comprises a data processing system. Chapter 1 has given you a good start on this.

To expand your expertise in computers, a good next step would be to pick up one or more of the excellent magazines being published on personal computing. These magazines vary in their subject complexity and intended audience—from rank beginner (you now) to expert (you in a couple of months). These magazines (several of which are listed at the end of this book) can be found at most computer stores and on many news-stands. Many of them offer both articles on computing and reviews of hardware and software. These reviews, along with your visits to computer stores and manufacturers' catalogs and product brochures, will be among your most valuable information resources. The advertisements in these magazines, as well as ones appearing in professional magazines such as the *Journal of Accountantcy*, are another valuable source. Most manufacturers of computer products are more than happy to send you reams of information on their products, and most will supply you with the locations of dealers who can answer any questions you might have about their products.

Computer stores are usually good places to visit. There you can see equipment from several manufacturers, and if any questions occur to you, most stores have salespeople who will be glad to answer them. Don't ever be afraid to ask a question for fear that you will look foolish. The field of personal computing is a new one, and the odds are very good that the salespeople you will be talking to are used to being asked questions you might feel are silly.

User groups are another inexpensive resource of vast use. These are organizations which may be concerned with one particular manufacturer's equipment (such as Apple Puget-sound Program Library Exchange—A.P.P.L.E., for short) or with a wider range of computers (such as the Boston Computer Society or New York Amateur Computer Club). Many user groups (which also have many potential users) have monthly meetings, publish newsletters, have hotlines to answer questions from their members, and offer access to software in the public domain. They are self-help organizations where members help each other and provide a good source to hear about other users' problems and experiences. Seminars run by professional societies, colleges, and even some computer stores are also a good source of information.

As you start to amass information on specific products, study it with your worksheets nearby. The worksheets will direct you to the information you are searching for and, as you find it, you will be able to fill in some (and eventually, most or all) of the blank spots and question marks on the various worksheets. For example, as you start to receive information on various types of general ledger software, you will be able to translate the capacities you previously estimated into a hardware capacity. As an example, suppose that you have located a general ledger package that you really like: it has all the features you need, you like the report formats, and so on. Reading the documentation you learn that the package has a capacity of 25 departments with 200 total accounts when used with a floppy disk-based system, and a capacity of 99 departments with an unlimited number of accounts when used with a hard disk-based system. Going back to your System Study Worksheet you find that a floppy-based system will not (with this particular piece of software) meet even your present needs, while a hard disk-based system will meet both present and anticipated future needs. You have just learned two important things. If you really want to use this particular software package, you will require a hard disk system. If you really don't want a hard disk system, you cannot use this particular software package.

Additionally, if the software specifications had listed the capacity as 200 accounts, no matter what the hardware configuration was, then you would have to judge the software as unusable regardless of how much you like the other features, as it fails to meet your minimum capacities required now.

As you continue in this manner, it will eventually become apparent to you what you will need in the way of hardware in order to run various software packages you have selected. There are two things to keep in mind during the data gathering phase. The first is that *software (rather than hardware) should be selected first.* Software, being the thing that "animates" an otherwise lifeless piece of machinery, is the prime consideration in the purchase of a computer system.

In some cases you will find a software package which is absolutely perfect for your use and find that it runs only on one particular manufacturer's system. In a case like this, if you decide you must have this particular piece of software, then you will be locked in to using a particular piece of hardware. This may further limit your choice of other application packages to those which run on the "locked-in" hardware. If this turns out to be so, it is best to be aware of it before you purchase anything! That is why software is usually selected first.

The second thing to keep in mind during the data gathering phase is that somewhere down the line, compromises will have to be made. If you are buying packaged software, you will probably have to settle for a package that is about 85–90%

of what your "dream" package would be. If you decide to write your own software or have a package customized, you will be trading off time and/or money against the convenience and economy of an off-the-shelf software package.

Until the 1970s almost all application software was custom-written. This is still true in many large computer installations. While in the last decide or so much packaged, off-the-shelf application software has become available for mainframe and minicomputers, the cost of such software has been prohibitive for the small businessman, many times running into the tens of thousands of dollars. The situation has changed considerably with the advent of personal computers. The availability of inexpensive computing resources has resulted in a virtual explosion in the marketing of inexpensive packaged software.

Many software packages running on personal computers have as many, if not more, features than those running on their bigger cousins. While the average cost of a general ledger which runs on a minicomputer is $5000 or more, it is possible to find excellent micro-based software packages with similar features for $500 to $1000. A problem which is common to packaged software in general, whether it runs on large or small equipment, is that no packaged software can satisfy all the needs of every user. There are four approaches to solving this problem. The first one is simply the compromise talked about earlier. You find the package that best serves your wants and needs, and live with whatever the limitations are. The second approach is to have the application custom-written from scratch. If the application is a fairly complex one, such as general ledger, it could easily take a year or more and tens of thousands of dollars to accomplish. On the plus side, chances are if the programmer you find for this task is competent, you will end up with software that closely resembles your specifications. Only you can decide whether the features missing from off-the-shelf software are worth paying 10 to 20 times the cost of a package.

A third solution is to purchase a software package and have it customized for you. While this seems like a reasonable approach, be aware that there are some not-so-obvious pitfalls in this. The first is that there are not many programmers competent enough to do a job like this. Even if the software is in a format that can be modified, a programmer must be able to analyze the software to determine what is being done at each and every point in the program. This by itself is no easy task. It consists of determining not only what is being done at each point in a program, but why it is being done. A programmer must then determine what changes have to be made to the software to add the features you desire and how making these changes will affect the rest of the software. I have seen cases where an apparently simple modification to a software program affected several other completely different functions in the software. An additional worry in using this approach is who will be responsible if a defect ("bug") shows up in the later use of the modified package. The more people involved in the creation of your "customized" package, the more people there are to point to each other and say, "It's his fault!" Typically, a manufacturer's warranty and support are rendered null by tampering with the package.

The fourth solution is to use an application/program generator and/or data base management software (DBMS) package. These software packages, described in greater detail in Chapter 10 on advanced applications, allow relatively unsophisticated computer users to develop their own custom programs and applications by essentially specifying what information has to go into the computer, what the computer should do with this information, and what the output (usually reports) should look like. This approach is an excellent one if the application is not too complex. The more complex the application is, the more expert you will have to become in the use both of this type of software and of computers.

There are several other points to keep in mind, whether your software is to be custom-written, customized, or purchased off the shelf. Documentation is the most often overlooked feature of a data processing system. That is, it is overlooked until it's needed. When you are selecting hardware and/or software, make sure the documentation (this includes manuals, users guides, etc.) is usable. By "usable" I mean not only readable and understandable, but readable and understandable at the level of the person who will be using the hardware/software. If this will be a member of your clerical staff (as it will be in many firms) then the documentation that will be used by that person should be free of "jargon" and "buzzwords," both computer- and accounting-oriented. The current trend toward "user-friendly" software (i.e., software that is menu-driven, does extensive error checking on input, and is largely self-explanatory) is fine as long as it works as it is supposed to (or as you expect it to), but if and when a problem crops up, your first line of recovery is the documentation supplied with the system. If the documentation is unusable, you will have to rely totally on the supplier or manufacturer. While this is not necessarily "the end of the world," realize that they will not necessarily feel the same sense of urgency in resolving your problem as you will.

If you decide to write your own software (or have it written or customized for you), the documentation issue becomes even more acute. As mentioned previously, a major problem with software is maintenance. With packaged software, maintenance is usually handled by the producer by way of issuing updates and/or upgrades to registered purchasers. When software has been written or modified for you, you can no longer rely on a single source to maintain it. The programmer who did the job may be unavailable or unwilling to correct any problems that crop up after the software is put into use. If you are the one who wrote or modified the software, you may not have the time needed, when needed. The solution to these potential problems is to insist on proper documentation standards no matter what the source of the software. Documentation standards are a complex subject in themselves, and I suggest that you get hold of one of the excellent books available on them. At a minimum, software should be documented on two levels, internal and external (although in many cases the internal documentation of packaged software will be inaccessible to the end user). Internal documentation consists of documentation contained in the program code itself (regardless of the computer language being used). This documentation details what program functions are being done at different sections of the program as well as any other information that a programmer who has never seen the program before would need in order to understand what is taking place in the program.

The second level of documentation, external documentation, exists itself on two levels. The first level of external documentation is called "application system level documentation" and consists of various written narrative and flowchart sheets detailing the construction of a program, what the program is supposed to do, and how it goes about doing it. The second level of external documentation is "user documentation." This consists of various narrative instructions to the user on how to load the program and how to use the program (e.g., for a report-printing program, how to go about getting the system to print the report).

THE OPERATING SYSTEM—THE COMPUTER'S INTERFACE WITH THE OUTSIDE WORLD

As your data gathering progresses you will eventually be coming across references to a feature of the computer called the "operating system." The *operating system* of a computer (and its attendant utility programs) is a piece of "system software" (as opposed to the specific "application software" we have been discussing) that allows the computer hardware to interact with the human operating it. To see how this works, let's imagine that you wish to run a program called "MENU" which lets you select from a variety of applications. Sitting at the keyboard, you type in "RUN MENU" (or just "MENU," depending on the particular operating system your computer uses). The computer hardware has no way of knowing what it is that you want done (remember—the computer "talks" internally in a machine language made up of numbers). The operating system, which is a program loaded when you turn the power on (this process is called "booting" the computer) reads the keyboard and interprets your instruction to "RUN MENU." These two words cause the operating system to go to the disk drive and check to see if a program called "MENU" is stored there. If it is, the operating system loads the program into the computer's RAM (random-access memory) and executes the program (causes it to run). If the operating system does not find a program called "MENU" on the disk, it will tell you so by printing a message such as "FILE NOT FOUND" on the console. As well as allowing the computer to interact with its human operator, the operating system also mediates between the computer and its peripherals (such as disk drive and printer). If a computer program wants to get or put a piece of data onto (or from) a disk file, it passes a request to the operating system which accesses the disk and reads or writes the data. If the program wants to output information to the printer, it passes a request to the operating system which sends the data to the printer. The operating system generally also contains various utilities. These are programs which format a disk (prepare a blank disk to store data), perform various copy functions (copy an individual file or an entire disk), and perform various helpful functions such as telling you what data are on a disk or how much room is left for new data.

Operating systems fall into two general categories: system-specific and non–system-specific. System-specific operating systems are provided by a manufacturer for his machine and his machine only. Programs written to run under a system-specific operating system will generally not be runable on the hardware from another manufacturer (nor will its data files be usable on a different manufacturer's equipment). Some examples of system-specific operation systems are Apple computer's DOS and SOS, Radio Shack's TRS-DOS, Commodore's Disk Operating System, and Atari's Disk Operating System. Many of these computers are also able to run a non–system-specific operating system, such as CP/M, although some computers may require an extra piece of hardware to do this.

Back in the "dark days" of microcomputing (the late 1970s), while many manufacturers were cranking out operating systems for their own machines, a company named Digital Research was developing an operating system that, with minor changes, would run on microcomputers using an 8080 chip for its CPU. This operating system, CP/M (which stands for control program for microcomputers), was later expanded to be able to run on systems using a more advanced chip in the same family, the Z-80 (and, more recently, Digital Research has introduced CP/M-86, which works on machines which use 16-bit chips such as the 8086 and 8088). CP/M is supplied, under license arrangement, as the "standard" operating system by many manufacturers. It is available from other sources for many computers whose manufacturers choose not to provide it. At this writing it is the most widely used operating system available for microcomputers. While this does not constitute an endorsement for CP/M, there are advantages to using a non–system-specific operating system rather than one which is system-specific. If you are using disk drives with the "standard" 8-inch, single-sided, single-density format, you can, in a pinch, use any other computer system running CP/M which uses the same disk format. This might give you an additional option in case of a computer system breakdown. In addition, if you are running CP/M on your system and decide to upgrade and/or acquire an additional system, you can be fairly confident that you will be able to use your software (though it may need some small modifications) with almost any computer that can run the CP/M operating system.

CP/M, while probably the best-known non–system-specific operating system, is not the only operating system that can be used on a variety of different hardware systems. Digital Research also offers MP/M, which is multiuser version of CP/M: it allows several terminals or CRTs to be used simultaneously on the same computer. Another non–hardware-specific operating system available to run on a variety of hardware is OASIS from Phase One. OASIS, like CP/M, is available in both single and multiuser versions. An additional operating system now becoming available in versions for personal computers is UNIX, which was developed by Bell Laboratories for use on large mini-computers.

While several multiuser operating systems are available, they should be considered only if the hardware is configured to support more than one user. Not all microcomputers are capable of this, and even with some that are, performance may start to degrade seriously with more than one user on the system. One of the greatest appeals of personal computers is the one-on-one relationship they encourage.

SOME CONSIDERATIONS REGARDING HARDWARE

As mentioned above, personal computing hardware has developed to the point where it is possible to buy a personal computer which has the capacity of supporting more than one user at a time. Multiuser systems usually do this in one of two ways. The first method used is "time-sharing." With this method, if the computer system has two users on it, it runs user 1's program for a little while (usually less than a second), then stores all that data and the program that user 1 was using and processes user 2's program and data. As a computer operates at great speeds, the individual user, on systems designed to operate in this manner, interacts with the computer as if she were the sole person using the system.

The second method used in multiuser systems on this level is "networking/resource sharing." In this setup, each user has her own individual computer. Each of these computers is connected to the other computers in the system, forming a network, which shares access to peripherals such as a high-capacity disk storage unit and a printer. Multiuser systems are fairly complex to configure and use. If you intend to implement this type of system, make sure that your dealer has extensive experience in multiuser hardware and software.

Another, potentially confusing hardware choice you will have to make is between the various disk storage devices available for personal computers. These high-capacity mass storage devices (detailed in Chapter 1) are available in "floppy" and "hard" versions with several sizes of each. Floppy disk drives use a flexible magnetically coated medium (hence "floppy") which is removable from the disk drive. They generally have smaller storage capacities than hard disks (in the range of 100,000 to 2,000,000 bytes or characters of storage). Hard disks, sometimes called "Winchester" disk drives (after the IBM code name for the first drive to use this particular drive technology) use a rigid, nonflexible, magnetic medium. Additionally, these rigid disks are sealed into the drive and are not removable. These drives offer storage capacities varying from 5 megabytes (5,000,000 characters of storage) to 80 megabytes or more. To further confuse the issue, several cartridge disk drives are available which use a rigid medium sealed into a removable cartridge. Which drive is best for your system will be decided by three factors: required capacity, access speed requirements, and, of course, finances.

In the process of converting the capacities listed on your System Study Worksheet into physical storage capacities (in characters or bytes) required by the various software packages you are evaluating, you will be able to determine whether you

FIGURE 5-1 A Floppy Disk.
Photos courtesy of IBM.

FIGURE 5-2 A Removable Cartridge Hard Disk

can use relatively inexpensive floppy storage or will require the considerably more expensive hard disk. For example, if the application software you choose does not require extensive storage capacity and you don't mind removing a diskette and replacing it with a different one to change clients or applications, then you probably can get along fine with the less expensive floppy disks. If, however, your application needs extensive storage capacity (for example, you might need to have on-line an entire year's general ledger transactions for a large client, say 15,000 or 20,000 transactions), or your application was "I/O-intensive," you would need the greater speed and storage capacity of a hard disk drive unit. *I/O-(input/output) intensive* applications are those that, because they require very large disk files, require very frequent disk access, either to read or write a disk record. Large inventories or payrolls are good examples of this type of application. I/O-intensive applications usually require hard disk units, not only because of their increased storage requirements, but also because the computer is able to read from and write to a hard disk at a much higher speed than to a floppy disk. While in many cases access speed is not a crucial factor, with programs (and applications) that require very frequent disk accesses, it may become so.

While at present, hard disks are several times more expensive than floppies, economies of scale and other factors, as manufacturers gain more experience, should bring the prices of hard disks down substantially.

One further consideration in the decision of what type of disk to use on your system is the problem of "backing up." *Backing up* is the process of making copies of your files and programs so that if something happens to the originals, you will lose no more data than those entered since your last backup was made. Backing up floppies is an easy task, especially with multiple-drive systems. Using a copy utility included with the operating system, you would just make a copy of your entire "original" disk. With high-capacity hard disks the procedure becomes a bit more complex. If you are backing up a 20-megabyte hard disk onto 1-megabyte floppies, then you would have to make transfers onto 20 floppies. There are two possible solutions to this problem. The first is to back up the entire hard disk once a month (it takes considerable time to back up onto 20 diskettes). Then, during the month, back up onto floppies just those files which have been changed since your last backup. For example, if a payroll file is used once a week, then it would be backed up once a week. This practice entails a bit of recordkeeping (you must keep track of which files are to be backed up at the end of the day), but should be a lot less trouble than backing up the entire hard disk every time you use the computer.

The second solution is to use a magnetic tape to back up, if available. Manufacturers and suppliers of hard disk units are aware of the backup problem. Some of them are offering high-speed tape units which allow an entire hard disk to be backed up onto tape in 15 or 20 minutes. If you decide you need (or want) a high-capacity hard disk, you may wish to see if you are able to purchase a compatible tape backup unit for the drive.

An additional controversy you are apt to run into concerns the type of CPU chip that various systems use. Currently popular machines use such diverse CPU chips as the 6502, 6809, 8080A, Z-80, Z8000, and the 68000. CPU chips are further classified as 8-bit chips or 16-bit chips. These 8- and 16-bit designations refer to the chip's *data bus width*, which is an indicator of how much RAM the CPU can directly address.

Many popular systems, such as the Apple II, Apple III, TRS-80 Models II and III, Xerox 820, and others use 8-bit CPU chips. Some of the more recent introductions, such as the IBM Personal Computer and the TRS-16, use 16-bit chips. At the present time there is not a tremendous performance difference between the 8-bit and 16-bit CPUs. Neither has the introduction of 16-bit equipment made obsolete the 8-bit equipment on the market. If the equipment you like uses a 16-bit CPU, that is fine. If it uses an 8-bit CPU, that is fine also.

The last two computer peripheral devices we will discuss in this chapter are video display terminals and printers. *Video display terminals* (VDTs), also called CRTs and "screens," are used to input information into and display information from the computer. They usually consist of a televisionlike screen and a typewriterlike keyboard. VDTs are available in "dumb" and "intelligent" models, the designation depending on the amount and type of features the terminal has. Some of the features you will find on the various terminals include numeric keypads and the ability to display information in different modes (such as reverse video) and at different intensities (brightnesses). More "intelligent" terminals have advanced editing features, internal memory storage, and the ability to program "special function keys" to send an entire command to the computer system by pressing a single key. While there is not a large price differential between most "dumb" and "intelligent" terminals, if the software you purchase does not make extensive use of "intelligent" features, chances are you won't either. Features you probably will find useful on any terminal include numeric keypads and different video display options such as reverse video and variable-intensity displays. Most packaged software is able to use these features, and they do ease the job of data entry.

Just as the VDT should be chosen with your uses in mind, your choice of printer will also be dependent on your uses. Plodding through your printer brochures, you will quickly discern that there are four terms used over and over in describing printers. The terms *letter-quality* and *draft-quality* are used to describe the appearance of the printed material, while *dot-matrix* and *daisy wheel* (or *thimble*) are terms used in describing the mechanism that produces the printed text.

Most printers used for business purposes are "impact"

printers; that is, they produce a letter on the paper by means of a character-producing mechanism pressing an inked ribbon against the paper. This is essentially the same mechanism your typewriter uses, where a key (or letter on a type ball or element) strikes the ribbon against the paper. The term *dot-matrix* is descriptive of a printer that uses a print head consisting of a number of sharp needles which are "fired" in a predetermined order and, pressing the ribbon to the paper, leave tiny dots of ink. Varying the firing order of the needles as the print head moves across the paper will determine the pattern of dots laid down (which result in different letters and numbers being printed). The density of the dot pattern laid down is described in terms of a "dot matrix," that is, number of dots high by number of dots wide. Generally, the more dots in the matrix, the denser the letter will appear and the less noticeable the dots themselves will be. Thus a printer using a 9×11 dot matrix will generally produce a less "dotty-looking" print than a printer using a 5×7 dot matrix.

The other type of printing mechanism used in printers for business applications uses a fully formed character. This letter, number, or symbol image is contained on an element which may resemble a golf ball, a disk with spokes (daisy wheel), or a thimble. The element is rotated to bring the correct letter into line with the paper and then is moved to press the ribbon against the paper. This produces the character in one impact against the paper (rather than the multiple impacts required by dot-matrix printers) and produces a fully formed character (rather than one made up of little dots).

Both types of printers have advantages and disadvantages. The dot-matrix printers are usually less expensive and work at greater speeds than "character" printers, which is a useful feature when you must print long reports such as a multiple-page general ledger. Letter-quality printers such as daisy wheel printers, while more expensive and much slower than dot-matrix printers, produce an exceptionally high-quality print. Which one is best depends on your use. If you produce reports and letters which must have a "quality" appearance, you will probably want a "character"-type printer. If appearance is not as important to you as volume, you probably will want a dot-matrix printer. Several dot-matrix printers offer an "enhanced-print" mode which essentially prints each letter twice, slightly offsetting the second printing. This produces a much denser print with less "dottiness" (although the print is still not letter-quality). This improvement in print quality is at the cost of greatly reduced print speed, but does produce a much nicer looking print than that normally associated with dot-matrix printers. Thus you could use "normal" print mode to produce long reports and switch to the "enhanced" mode when you wished to produce a document which required a "nicer" appearance.

```
THIS IS A SAMPLE PRINTED ON A NEC 5510 SPINWRITER(TM) LETTER-QUALITY PRINTER
THIS IS A SAMPLE PRINTED ON A NEC 5510 SPINWRITER(TM) LETTER-QUALITY PRINTER
THIS IS A SAMPLE PRINTED ON A NEC 5510 SPINWRITER(TM) LETTER-QUALITY PRINTER
THIS IS A SAMPLE PRINTED ON A NEC 5510 SPINWRITER(TM) LETTER-QUALITY PRINTER
THIS IS A SAMPLE PRINTED ON A NEC 5510 SPINWRITER(TM) LETTER-QUALITY PRINTER
THIS IS A SAMPLE PRINTED ON A NEC 5510 SPINWRITER(TM) LETTER-QUALITY PRINTER
```

```
SAMPLE DOT-MATRIX PRINT : EPSON MX-80(TM) IN REGULAR PRINT MODE

SAMPLE DOT-MATRIX PRINT : EPSON MX-80(TM) IN REGULAR PRINT MODE

SAMPLE DOT-MATRIX PRINT : EPSON MX-80(TM) IN REGULAR PRINT MODE


SAMPLE DOT-MATRIX PRINT : EPSON MX-80(TM) IN DOUBLE STRIKE MODE

SAMPLE DOT-MATRIX PRINT : EPSON MX-80(TM) IN DOUBLE STRIKE MODE

SAMPLE DOT-MATRIX PRINT : EPSON MX-80(TM) IN DOUBLE STRIKE MODE
```

FIGURE 5-3 An Example of "Letter-Quality," Regular Dot-Matrix, and Double-Strike Dot-Matrix Print

An additional development which may influence your choice of printers is the entrance of several typewriter manufacturers into the computer printer market. At this writing several "low-end" daisy wheel printers have been introduced which have retail prices of $1000 or less. While generally not suitable for use as your only printer because of their extremely slow speed (around 12 characters per second), you may want to consider one of these units as a second printer for your system. That way you could use the fast dot-matrix printer for a majority of your printing needs and switch to the daisy wheel printer when you needed letter-quality print.

6

CHOOSING HARDWARE AND SUPPLIES

The preceding chapter covered many of the details that should be considered in choosing personal computer software and hardware. By this point you should have a fairly good idea of what your needs are and what will be required in the way of software and hardware to satisfy them. This chapter will touch on several other considerations pertaining to both the choice of hardware and supplies.

One thing that quickly becomes obvious as the hardware brochures start to pile up is that while there may be close to a hundred manufacturers, the functional specifications of much of the equipment are very similar. This, of course, does nothing to make your choice any easier.

Manufacturers of personal computer equipment generally fall into one of three categories. The greatest number of manufacturers are the "newcomers." These are companies that have been producing personal computers for a year or two. Many of these companies will be out of business in the next year or two. This is an unfortunate fact of life and is, in many cases, a result of our economic times and not a reflection on the quality of any one piece of hardware. Many of the original pioneering firms in the microcomputer field have folded (but then again, so have some very large established companies).

The next group of manufacturers are the "old-timers no one has ever heard of." These are companies that have been turning out microcomputers since the late 1970s. They are still around because they make excellent equipment, but they are relatively unknown because they don't seem to have the flash, and the advertising budget, of the better-known companies.

This brings us to the last group, the "big names in personal computers." These companies actually fall into two subgroups, the "brand names" who started out in the personal computer field such as Apple, Radio Shack, Commodore, and a few others, and the "big computer" companies which have more recently started producing personal computers. The most famous of these is, of course, "Big Blue," IBM, but most of the other large computer manufacturers such as Xerox, Hewlett-Packard, and Digital Equipment Corporation (DEC) have already announced, or are expected to announce, their own personal-size systems.

A prospective buyer's first impulse is to go with a "brand name" system. Manufacturers spend millions of dollars a year to instill this reflex in the buyer. Brand name recognition, however, should not be your primary consideration. As a newcomer to the field of personal computing, chances are you will need a fair amount of hand holding. Most manufacturers support their products primarily through their dealer network. There is nothing wrong with this, but it pays to give some thought to how a problem would be handled if the dealer were unable (or unwilling) to assist you in resolving a problem (or even if the dealer went out of business). Many computer manufacturers, though by no means all, provide a measure of "backup" support to the end user (you!).

Additionally, a great deal of thought should be given to the maintainability of your system. If a dealer tries to tell you that a personal computer will never break down, take the opportunity to remind him that the only things certain in this life are death and taxes (although someday we all may live forever). One of Murphy's laws states that a computer system will only break down at the exact moment it is most inopportune. Find out who fixes what, how long particular repairs take, and the costs involved. Some companies offer extended warranties on carry-in service for an additional charge.

You must decide how long, under worst-case circumstances, you can afford to be without the use of your system. It is now possible to obtain maintenance contracts for on-site service (just like that offered on larger systems). Some companies offer this service themselves, and some contract with nationwide service companies such as SORBUS, RCA, and GE Service. While on-site maintenance contracts are expensive in relation to the price of the system, they generally are worth it if you feel that you cannot (or do not want to) be without the use of your system for more than a day. The length of time needed to effect repairs on a "carry-in" basis varies from 24 hours (from IBM) to possibly weeks. The time to find out about this is now, before you buy, and not when one of your pieces of equipment gives up the ghost.

This leads us into a related area of consideration—where to buy the equipment. In your earlier research you have no doubt noticed, in reading the mail-order ads in various computer magazines, that the exact same piece of equipment is being sold at prices varying from list price (or more) to 30% or 40% below list. While I am probably the last person in the world to advise someone to squander their money, I would like to leave you with just two thoughts on this matter. The first is the old saying, "You get what you pay for." Generally, I have found this to be true. When you are paying list price, you are not only buying a product, you are also purchasing a measure of support of that product from the dealer.

Secondly, I have occasionally had trouble getting a dealer to support a product which I have purchased at list price. As a next-to-last resort (the last being my attorney), I have sometimes had good results waiting until a Saturday with a large crowd in the store and complaining, loudly but politely, about the degree of after-sale support the store is providing. The more people in the store at the time, the more effective this technique seems to be. While I have not had to resort to this very often, it seems reasonable to believe that this technique would not achieve as much when used with a company accessible only by mail or phone.

An additional area to give some thought to before plunking down the dollars concerns purely physical considerations. These include the physical size and layout of the equipment, where the equipment will be located in your office, and storage

LADELLE M. HYMAN

of records, files, and supplies. An additional factor to consider is who will be using the system. Will access be restricted, and if so, how? Physical size and location of the equipment may not be major considerations, but if you intend to have the computer on your desk, you may want to consider a one- or two-piece system rather than a system comprised of nine or ten pieces with cables running all around. Additionally, while personal computers no longer require special, air-conditioned environments, they should still be located in a clean place with adequate air circulation. Floppy disks are sensitive to dust and dirt and should be used in a relatively clean area. Heat buildup is an enemy of all electronic equipment, including your computer. While your system will not burn up if used in a location where the heat generated by it cannot dissipate, this type of use will most likely result in more repairs and maintenance being required over the life of the system.

Give some thought, also, to storage requirements. Where will you store client printouts and records kept on diskettes? Paper supplies should be stored in relatively dry locations, as they tend to absorb moisture, which can lead to feeding problems when printing.

Who in the office will be using the system? If the computer will be used by many people in your firm, then it should be located in a position convenient to frequent changes of personnel. If access is to be restricted, how will this be done? There are many ways of restricting access to information. Some of these include putting the system in a locked room, electrically locking the system (this requires a key to turn the system on like the ignition key to your car), using software which uses password protection to restrict access to programs and information, and keeping information contained on floppy disks under lock and key. If you intend to use one one or more of these techniques, be sure that the hardware and software you are considering will support the technique you wish to use.

An additional factor involved in the consideration of who is to use the system is that of training. Training involves two separate fields of operation. The user must first be trained to operate the hardware. While in some instances this may involve no more than turning one switch on and off, some computer hardware may require considerably more effort to use. The second area of training involves both system software (the operating system and utilities) and application software. The operation of a "spreadsheet" program may be quite different from the operation of a write-up program. Who will do the training? Will the supplier train everyone in your firm? Will they train one person who will then (hopefully) pass on the knowledge? Are your people expected to teach themselves from the manuals, and if this is the case, are they capable of doing so? If you have only one person to do the operations, what happens if they quit or are out sick? Plan now and you will be ready should the need ever arise. If the supplier is to provide training, make sure that the extent and duration are spelled out in the sales contract and, if additional training should be needed, that the availability and price of these are also spelled out in writing.

The last item we will consider in this chapter is "hidden costs." In purchasing a computer (or most other things) many of the costs are up front and obvious. A disk drive costs this amount, a printer that amount. There are some costs involved that may not be quite as obvious, and, while they probably will not affect your decision to purchase a particular system, you should be aware that they exist. These hidden costs consist of items such as supplies, furniture, electrical work, and the opportunity costs of training personnel, and can range from the trivial to the considerable.

A computer, no matter how complete or self-contained, will require additional supplies to be used. A computer which is floppy disk–based, or hard disk–based using floppy disks for backup, will reqire that you purchase a supply of diskettes. These are manufactured by many companies and are available from your dealer, computer supply companies such as Visible Computer Supply and Inmac, and many office supply companies (such as Ginn's). They range in price from $2 to $10 each depending on manufacturer, size and capacity, and quantity ordered. If you anticipate using many of them you will be best off purchasing in lots of 100 or more.

Using your printer will require a supply of paper and ribbons. Paper is available in a myriad of sizes, plys, and weights. Most often used sizes include 9.5 × 11 inches with perforations on the edges that allow the pin-feed perforations to be torn off, reducing the sheet to regular letter size (8.5 × 11 inches), and 14.5×11 inches. The smaller (9.5×11) paper is most often used when the printout is 80 columns or less wide, while the larger sheet size (14.5 × 11) can accommodate 132 columns (or more at a smaller print pitch) of information. Computer paper is commonly available in 15-pound weight, although I prefer to use a heavier (18- or 20-pound) paper when I can find it (the heavier paper seems to feed through the printer and to stack better). Ribbons for printers are usually available in two types, film and fabric. The film ribbon feeds once through the printer and then must be replaced, while the fabric ribbon can be used until the print becomes light enough to be objectionable. The ribbons for many printers come in easily changed cartridges. I tend to use both film and fabric ribbons, the film (single-use) when I use the system for word processing tasks or want to produce a printout for a client, and the fabric for general-purpose use such as printing client general ledgers that will remain at my office. Paper and ribbons are available from the sources mentioned above as well as some manufacturers who sell directly to the user.

Three additional hidden costs that you should be aware of are furniture, electrical work, and opportunity costs of training. While personal computers need no special furniture, you may wish to buy one of the many computer desks on the market. These are desks designed to hold the various components of a computer in a neat and organized manner. Additionally, many have storage facilities built in to store floppy disks and manuals close at hand (and they look great!). Personal computers also do not need special electrical outlets. Most draw no more power than one or two desk lamps. They should not, however, be used on the same electrical line as heavy machinery (such as a refrigerator, copier, or power tools), as these devices are capable of throwing electrical "noise" onto the line which can affect the sensitive circuits inside the computer. Computers are sensitive to static electricity, and if this is a problem in your office, or if your office is carpeted, you may want to use a conductive mat (such as 3M's Velostat) in the area around your system to preclude damage or loss of data.

If the location of your system is not near an electric outlet, you may want to consider having a new outlet installed. Not only is it much neater than using an extension cord, but it lessens the chance of someone accidentally tripping on the cord and pulling out the plug just as your operator has finished entering the last of 500 entries.

The last cost to be discussed in this chapter is the opportunity cost of training. This is the cost of having your staff learn to use the computer when they could be doing something else. There is not much that can be done about this except to be aware of it and try to schedule staff training (and the installation of the computer) at a time when the staff would normally have some slack or free time.

7

ACQUISITION AND INSTALLATION

By this time you should have a fairly good idea of your computer requirements and what will be needed in the way of hardware and software to meet them. This chapter will focus on the factors you should be aware of during the acquisition and installation phases. The source of your system is conceivably as important a consideration as the hardware and software itself. While I have expressed my feelings about buying through mail order or discounters earlier in this book, there are several additional points I would like to bring up at this point. Personal computer hardware, when purchased new, is covered for varying lengths of time by the manufacturer's warranty. This warranty is, in most cases, administered by the dealer from whom you purchased the equipment. Unless you have contracted for on-site maintenance from the day the equipment is delivered, you will have to return the equipment to the dealer for any repairs or exchanges within the warranty period. If the dealer you purchased the system from is a considerable distance away, any problems you might have could incur considerable costs in terms of both money and the time you are without the use of your computer. If this is beginning to sound like an ad for "buy local" and "get a service contract," you are right. I consider both of these as forms of insurance. I don't intend to sound pessimistic about the reliability of personal computers. In my experience they have proven to be extremely reliable, rugged pieces of equipment. I do feel, though, that if you have the opportunity to anticipate trouble, you will be much better prepared in the event trouble appears. Many of the computer manufacturers themselves have expressed concern over the ability of discounters and mail-order retailers to provide good after-sale support.

There are some slightly different considerations necessary in the decision of where to buy software. This is largely because of the nature of software. Except for the medium it is provided on, software is an intangible. Software producers realize this and specifically disclaim all warranties (including, in many cases, implied warrantee of merchantability) except for replacement of media. Add to this the fact that easily 75% to 80% of all the software being sold today is junk (although, thankfully, this seems to be on the decrease) and you have the perfect situation for *caveat emptor* ("let the buyer beware"). It is possible to save money buying software through mail order if you follow several basic rules:

1. Know what you are buying. If it is at all possible, try to have the software demonstrated to you locally (although this is a terrible thing to do to a dealer).

2. Try to stick to "name brand" software when buying software from a distant or not easily accessible source.

3. Try to deal with a mail-order dealer who has been around for a while. Examine the back issues of computer magazines to check on this. You may also want to to call the Better Business Bureau in the town where the company is based. If you are a member of a user group, ask if any other members have had dealings with your supplier.

4. Don't expect the same amount of after-sale support you might get from a local dealer. This support is often provided for in the local dealer's price (which is why buying locally is usually more expensive than buying through mail order).

The purchase and maintenance of software is one place a consultant, if you decide to engage one, can be very useful. He should be able to direct you to a reputable mail-order firm as well as discuss the pros and cons of various software packages you might be considering. As a last resort, you can always turn to the producer of the software, though, as a rule, they are not generally responsive in dealing with end users. Some manufacturers, however, are concerned about the support the end users have been getting from their dealers. Recently, several manufacturers of software have set up technical hotlines to answer questions from their end users. This is a good sign, but whether or not this will become widespread remains to be seen.

Financing is another factor which will help determine where you buy the hardware. As an accountant, you are in the best position to know which is the best method of acquisition for your circumstances. What you may wish to do, if your dealer offers it, is a "trial marriage." This is a short-term lease (usually a year) with the option to purchase the system at the end of the term and have part of the lease payments applied to the purchase price. While your lease payments will probably be quite a bit more than a bank loan payment for an outright purchase, this option gives you the opportunity to "get your feet wet" without a large cash outlay or long-term commitment. If the equipment proves unsuitable, you are only stuck with it for the duration of the lease term. This benefit also holds true for the dealer and gives you the opportunity to find out what you can expect in the way of support from him. If he is unsupportive during the lease period, you can imagine the amount of support you will see once he has the purchase amount in hand.

Recently, some dealers have started to supply personal computers on straight rental with rental periods as short as three months. This is convenient if you are leaning toward a particular system but are really unsure if it will serve your needs.

While several years ago the only way to finance a personal computer was with a personal loan, many banks and leasing companies are now willing to write leases on this type of equipment. Additionally, several manufacturers have either set up their own leasing companies or made "blanket" arrangements with leasing companies to enable purchasers of equipment to finance their systems. Many dealers also have arrangements with independent leasing companies or local banks to give their customers "extra" attention. While most of the leases offered now are financing leases, it is not unreasonable to expect that more operating leases will be written as the leasing companies gain more experience with the personal computer equipment market. Additionally, many leasing companies will "pass-through" the investment tax credit if requested, although the lease term will affect the amount that can be taken.

Assuming that you have chosen a computer, some packaged software, and a dealer, the next step is to buy your system. If you are making an outright purchase (either paying for it out of pocket or arranging your own loan), then the sales contract is usually nothing more than a bill of sale conveying title in the property received to you. If you are leasing the equipment through a third-party leasing company and/or purchasing the system with customized or custom-written software, the situation becomes a bit more complex. In a third-party lease, the leasing company is buying the hardware and software from the dealer and leasing it to you. In this situation, the leasing company may ask for a "letter of intent" or may require that the lease papers be signed before the system is ordered. A *letter of intent* is usually a simple note on your letterhead that you intend to lease a particular configuration of hardware and/or software from the leasing company. As this may or may not be a legal commitment, it pays to discuss this with your attorney. He may suggest additional items that should be in the letter of intent such as the lease rate and payment amount of the lease.

If the leasing company insists that the lease agreement be signed before the equipment is ordered, make sure you do not return the "signoff" sheet or release until satisfied. You will find this sheet somewhere in the packet of lease papers. It usually states something to the effect that you have received delivery of the equipment in working order and that you release the leasing company from any and all responsibility. It also authorizes the leasing company to pay the supplier for the equipment. Under no circumstance should this be signed until you are certain that *all* the equipment and software has been supplied to you and is working properly!

Lease papers are a legal contract between you and the leasing company. Always have them examined by your attorney before signing them. Make certain that the terms stated in the agreement are the ones you have agreed to. Check the lease term, rate of interest, and monthly payment for correctness. If the leasing company has agreed to pass-through the investment tax credit, be certain this is set down in writing in the agreement. If you have a buy-out option at the end of the lease, make sure that this fact and the terms of the buy-out are detailed in the lease agreement.

Financing becomes even more confused when you are purchasing (or leasing) both hardware and customized or custom-written software from the same dealer as part of a package. A problem sometimes arises in these circumstances because the hardware part of the purchase may be installed and operating long before the software is. Unless your financing or leasing agreement provides for partial payments to the dealer, he will either get the entire amount due him even if he has not supplied working software (if you sign off the system) or nothing (if you do not sign off the system).

The solution to this problem is to include as part of the lease agreement (or sales agreement if you are financing the system) a software contract similar to that discussed in the next chapter. This should provide for progressive payments upon demonstrable milestones and should include an installation schedule and penalty provisions for unreasonable delays or nonperformance. This contract should be agreed to by all parties to the transaction, including the leasing company, if the equipment is to be leased. Some leasing companies will refuse to become involved in a situation that requires partial sign-offs. In this case you will either have to find a leasing company that will accept these terms, or the dealer will have to agree to wait until everything has been delivered to see any money (this is highly unlikely), or a third party must be involved.

In the case of a third-party involvement the leasing company releases the entire amount of money (for both hardware and software) to an agreed-upon third party who will hold it in escrow and release partial payments to the supplier upon demonstrable milestones. This will usually be the most practical approach to situations where the entire system (hardware and software) will not be installed at the same time. You will probably have to bear the extra cost involved, but in most cases the extra protection and leverage this method affords (over a straight sign-off) is worth the extra cost. If this method is selected, make certain that the lease agreement provides for payments into escrow upon your sign-off to them. You will also have to execute a separate contract with the computer dealer which, along with the other details discussed in this and the following chapter, will also include an installation schedule.

THE INSTALLATION SCHEDULE

In many cases, the installation of a personal computer system consists of nothing more than unpacking the equipment, reading the manuals, plugging in some plugs, and inserting some disks. There are some circumstances where the installation becomes a bit more involved. This can be the result of a complex configuration of hardware, the use of customized or custom-written software, or an agreement with the dealer to hook up your system and train your people in its use. In situations such as these, the use of an installation schedule, as an adjunct to the software contract, is a good idea.

The *installation schedule* is an extension of the milestone method used in software contracts. Rather than being limited to one application software system, the installation schedule is concerned with the installation of an entire facility, from delivery of the equipment to training, debugging, and final sign-off. The document gives completion dates for achievement of certain capabilities called ("milestones") and states the amount of escrow that will be released to the dealer upon reaching these milestones. This document is then signed or initialed by the dealer and you and becomes a part of the formal software contract or sales agreement.

An example of an Installation Schedule is illustrated in Fig. 7-1. In this example, the practitioner has purchased a complete "package" consisting of hardware, custom software, packaged software, and installation and training of her operator in the use of both the off-the-shelf software and the custom application. The cost of the package is $11,200.00 which breaks down as follows:

1. Hardware $5500.00
2. Packaged software $700.00
3. Custom software $4000.00
4. Installation and training $1000.00

INSTALLATION SCHEDULE

Date	Action
11/1/8X	All equipment and packaged software delivered.
11/3/8X	Hardware unpacked, assembled, and tested. Hardware will be fully operational. (Payment of $6200.00 released from escrow)
11/8/8X	Operator training on use of hardware, operating system, and packaged software will be finished. (Payment of $1000.00 released from escrow.)
11/19/8X	Data entry and file maintenance features of custom software package installed on system and demonstrated. (Payment of $1000.00 released from escrow.)
11/29/8X	Remainder of custom software installed on system and demonstrated. (Payment of $1000.00 released from escrow.)
12/6/8X	Operator training on custom software will be completed. (Payment of $2000.00 released from escrow.)
12/31/8X	Parallel run completed. System performing as per agreed upon specifications. *Final sign-off.* (Payment of $3000.00 released from escrow.)

AGREED

Signature _____; *Client*

Signature _____; *Dealer*

FIGURE 7-1 Example: Installation Schedule

The practitioner and dealer agree that the installation will take place over a two-month period, which will include a parallel run for one period with their currently used manual system. Both agree on the milestones to be demonstrated, the amounts to be paid at each milestone, and the third party who will hold the money in escrow and disburse the funds. Other matters pertaining to the software contract (discussed in next chapter), such as penalties for missing a scheduled date, what length of time will be allowed as a grace period, and nonperformance (poor performance) remedies, are agreed upon and are included in the software contract (not the installation schedule). The installation schedule is prepared, initialed, and incorporated into the software contract. The milestones and dates were established as follows (assume that today's date is 10/1/8X):

11/1/8X—Deliver equipment and packaged software: This is set at one month as the dealer does not have all the equipment in stock and must obtain some of it from his distributor.

11/3/8X—Hardware fully operational: The dealer agrees to come over the day after delivery (11/2/8X), set up the equipment, and insure that everything is working properly. An extra day (to 11/3) is built in, in case any adjustments are needed as a result of shipping. It is agreed that when the dealer can demonstrate that the packaged software runs with no problems on the equipment, a payment of $6200.00 will be released from escrow. This amount covers the purchase price of the equipment and the packaged software. At this point in the installation the dealer has delivered a working system (although not the *complete* system in terms of the contract) and has been paid for what has been delivered.

11/8/8X—Operator training: The dealer and accountant agree that operator training should be done in two phases. Phase 1 will acquaint the operator with the equipment and packaged software, while phase 2 will concentrate on the custom software. As the custom software is not scheduled to be delivered until a month after the equipment is installed, the operator will have sufficient time to become familiar with the operation of the packaged software. The dealer estimates that two days' training will be sufficient for phase 1. At the completion of the phase 1 training a payment of $1000.00 will be released from escrow—$500.00 for the training and a $500.00 retainer toward the custom programming. (*Note:* The five-day gap between 11/3 and 11/8 reflects a weekend between the two dates.)

11/19/8X—First half of custom software installed and demonstrated: The dealer and accountant agree that demonstration of data entry and file maintenance functions of the custom software shall constitute the next milestone. While this constitutes approximately half of the contracted for software, only a payment of $1000.00 will be released at this time. The additional amount that would normally be paid the dealer at this time (custom software = $4,000.00 $\times$ $\frac{1}{2}$ = $2000.00) will be deferred until final sign-off to insure that the dealer has a financial stake in correcting any problems that crop up before the final sign-off.

11/29/8X—Remainder of custom software is installed and demonstrated: Again, only $1000.00 payment is released from escrow at this point for the same reason as when the first half of the software was installed.

12/6/8X—Operator training on custom software (phase 2 training) is completed: The dealer and accountant have allowed for six days of operator training on the custom software. The dealer is charging $500.00 per day for this training. Upon achieving this milestone, payment of $2000.00 will be released from the escrow account with the additional $1000.00 deferred to final sign-off.

12/31/8X—Final sign-off: Both parties agree that after the custom software has been installed and the operator trained, they will run in parallel with their manual system for three weeks. If at the end of this three-week run the system is performing as per agreed upon specifications, and if any "bugs" that have shown up have been corrected, the system will be "signed off" and the remainder of the money held in escrow will be paid to the dealer.

This example has demonstrated how an installation schedule is developed. There are several points to keep in mind when developing an installation schedule. The milestones that you and the dealer agree upon should be readily identifiable occurrences. If these milestones are vaguely defined, there is a good chance that the two of you will disagree, somewhere down the line, about whether a milestone has been met. A second point is to try to find a balance in the number of milestones established. If there are too few, the dealer may feel resentful at having to wait for payment he feels he is entitled to. Too many milestones, on the other hand, will drive everyone crazy—you, the dealer, and the third party handling the escrow payments.

The last point to keep in mind regarding installation schedules is their purpose. The installation schedule and its adjunct, the software contract, exist to provide both you and the dealer with legal assurances that each of you will provide what has been promised. On the dealer's part this consists of any hardware and software that have been purchased and/or contracted for. On your part, the dealer has been assured that he will be paid, in a fair and timely manner, as long as he delivers what has been promised, when it is promised. Bear in mind that there is usually a tendency to underestimate the length of time a task will take. Try to be realistic when setting milestones. If you pressure the dealer into promising equipment and/or software in an unreasonably short time period, you are just looking for problems down the line. To accomplish anything well takes time. If you allow for this, chances are good that both you and the dealer will be pleased with the transaction when the installation has been completed.

8

SOFTWARE: FURTHER CONSIDERATIONS

While there are a multitude of application software packages available "off the shelf," it is quite possible that you may have an application in mind for which there is no package available. Perhaps you have found a package which meets your needs but lacks a particular feature you would really like to have. There are several solutions to this problem. If the application is not too complex, you might consider using a data base management system or application/program generator. This type of software is detailed in Chapter 10. Another approach is to have the software custom-written or a commercially available package customized.

If you decide on this solution, the next decision you will have to make is how you will go about having the software written (or customized). There are several ways to go about having software customized or custom-written for you. If your application is very complex or you anticipate requiring a large amount of customized software, you should consider adding a programmer to your staff. This in-house approach will have several benefits. It gives you unlimited access to the programmer's skills. Furthermore, while you may not be able to reliably estimate the total end cost of the software, you will have the advantage of paying for the software over a period of time (the length of employment on the project) and at a known rate (the programmer's salary, plus benefits and payroll taxes).

While this sounds like the ideal approach, there are some disadvantages to doing things this way. Skilled programmers are rare and command high salaries. If you are able to locate one who suits your needs, it is unlikely that he would be interested in a full-time job of limited duration. A programmer on your payroll receiving a weekly salary has little incentive to finish the job in as short a time as possible. This is further complicated by the inability of most office managers (who would be the programmer's direct supervisor) to judge the level of production of a programmer. One possible approach, if you feel that you would like to have an in-house programming staff but do not necessarily need someone on a full-time basis (and are not time-constrained as to implementation of custom programming projects), is to hire a programmer on a part-time basis. A good source of part-time programming help is a local college or university with a computer science program. Many schools will cooperate with you in developing an internship or work–study program.

This approach yields several benefits. Part-time programming help from this source is usually inexpensive due to the students' lack of "real-world" experience. This lack of experience is not necessarily the minus point it might first appear. Most college students working part-time in this capacity are highly motivated. They are, for the most part, grateful to be working "in the field" and being paid, as well as gaining experience. Moreover, they will be able to, in many cases, call on the resources and experience of their professors if they should run into a problem. Of course, many of the disadvantages of going "in-house" remain whether your staff is full-time or part-time.

A second approach to custom software is to contract for it with outside sources. These can include computer dealers, system houses, and contract programmers.

System houses are companies which specialize in software for vertical markets. This means that they pick one or more specific markets (such as accountants, lawyers, doctors, etc.) and specialize in software for that (or those) market(s). Contract programmers are individuals or companies which specialize in writing or customizing software according to previously agreed-upon specifications. The line between contract programmers and system houses is a blurred one. A company calling itself a "systems house" is more likely to specialize in a particular market, but both perform the same function—the development of custom software. Additionally, many consulting firms in the data processing field will also contract to do custom software work. If you are having a software package customized for you, you should try to contact the manufacturer of the package. In some cases, if the producer of the software feels that your modification would be well received in the marketplace, he may undertake producing the modified package himself. If the producer is not interested in doing the modifications, he may be able to recommend someone who is familiar with the software to do the customizing.

There are several potential problems in having software modified that you should be aware of. The most likely problem, the difficulty of the task, has already been discussed. It may, in fact, be more difficult for a programmer to modify someone else's software than for him to write the desired end product from scratch. Thus, it is quite possible that it would cost more, both in time and money, to have a packaged piece of software modified than to have it custom-written. A second potential problem is that the software package you desire to be modified may not be available in a form that can be modified. Some manufacturers, fearful of their products being pirated (copied and sold illegally), provide their software in a "locked" format that prevents the software from being copied or listed. If the software cannot be listed, it cannot be modified. Many manufacturers do not want their software to be modified or tampered with, as it is often possible that a modification will adversely affect other parts of the software. Another method manufacturers use to prevent tampering is to provide the software in machine language format (this is also called "compiled" or "assembled" code). This makes it extremely difficult, if not impossible, for a programmer not intimately familiar with the particular piece of software to understand and analyze what is taking place in the program. If a programmer is not able to make this analysis, she will not be able to modify the program.

Assuming that you are able to have modifications made or that you will have software written for you, the next item to consider is the software specification. This is a document that sets forth in exact detail precisely what the modified or custom-written software is supposed to do and how the software will do it. If packaged software is being modified, then the specification document will detail what modifications will be made and what the effects of the modifications will be. For example, if the only modification you are having done is to add an additional report to a packaged application system, the specification document would detail what the report would look like (and should contain a mock-up of the report), how the report is to be accessed (is the access from the application system menu or from the operating system?), and what happens when the report is finished running (does the system return to the application system menu or exit to the operating system?).

The specification document becomes much more complex when software is being custom-written. This is because the software exists only in your imagination and mind. As you cannot reasonably expect a programmer to be able to read your mind, anything and everything you expect to have at the end of the project should be detailed. The specification document would normally be produced by the programmer, but should not be accepted by you until you are satisfied that it describes exactly what you expect out of the finished product. This specification document will become part of the contract between you and the producer. Do not accept verbal assurances. Remember that "if it isn't in writing, it isn't."

The specification document will most likely contain a narrative description of the program or programs, flowcharts of the programs, disk file layouts, what data will be required for input and samples of data entry display screens, and samples of reports produced. The specification should also contain anything else that you feel you would like to have in writing. Once you are satisfied with the specification document, the next step is contracting for the job. Any time a major amount of work is being done (over a few hundred dollars), always insist on a contract. This is for your protection as well as insuring that the contractor will be paid if the job meets specifications. This contract, which may be in the form of an engagement letter, should be a legally binding document, and as such should be examined by your attorney before you sign it. Most software professionals have a more or less standard contract that they use. If your contract programmer can't supply this document, ask your attorney to draft an agreement for you. In either case, the agreement and its supporting specification document should spell out what you expect to get, when you expect to get it, what it will cost, and what remedies are available for poor performance or nonperformance. In addition, the contract should set out the extent of ownership of the software. Both a sample software contract and parts of a specification document are illustrated in Appendix D.

Software, being an intangible, is subject to varying degrees and forms of ownership and use. The most obvious of these is an outright purchase of the software. The programmer relinquishes to you his entire interest and rights to the software. He cannot keep, use, or sell the software to anyone else. You have the right to use or dispose of the software in any manner you see fit. This type of transfer cannot take place with modification of packaged software unless the person modifying the package has exclusive rights to the original, unmodified software. If not, the most that he can transfer to you are his interests and right to the modifications. Other forms of purchase arrangements include a sale to you where the programmer retains the right to resale and where both of you have the right to resale. These sales contracts may also contain nondisclosure agreements and convenants restricting competition or limiting the markets each of you can sell to. If the software is to be copyrighted, the contract should set forth who will own the copyrights.

A common occurrence in the software world is the user license. With much of the packaged software being sold today you are not purchasing a copy of the software. What you are purchasing is a nonexclusive license to use the software, generally for a fixed period of time. There are many other forms of licensing arrangements, including exclusive and restricted user licenses and exclusive and nonexclusive licenses to sell. If your software contract contains licensing provisions, be sure you are aware of the rights and obligations the license puts you under. For example, some licenses give you exclusive use of custom-written software but contain nondisclosure agreements prohibiting you from letting anyone else see the program code. If you have obtained custom software under this type of agreement and wanted further modifications made, you would have to go back to the original author for those modifications. The nondisclosure agreement in the license would prohibit you from bringing in someone new to further modify the program.

The moral of all this is twofold: know what it is that you are buying, and make sure you know exactly what it is that you are agreeing to when you sign a contract.

Other features a contract should cover are duration of the project, milestones, and payments. Generally custom-written software takes a while to produce. You and your programmer should agree upon both a delivery date and a grace period. There should be penalties for nondelivery beyond the grace period and a mechanism for settling disputes. As an example of how this works, let's suppose that you have contracted with Joe Programmer to write a depreciation reporting system. You and Joe agree that the system shall be due 90 days after the contract is signed with a 30-day grace period. You further agree that the system shall be considered delivered when Joe can, on your system, demonstrate that all features detailed in the specification document work as per the specification document. You agree to pay Joe $3000 for all rights to the software and that payment shall be made in three payments of $1000 each. The first $1000 will be due at the signing of the contract, the second $1000 when Joe can demonstrate certain agreed-upon features, and the last $1000 will be due when the system is delivered. You and Joe also agree that disputes will be resolved by arbitration according to the rules of the American Arbitration Association. You and Joe further agree that if Joe cannot deliver the system before the end of the grace period, the last payment will be reduced by $100 for each week past the grace period that Joe fails to deliver. If by the tenth week past the grace period Joe is still unable to deliver, he must repay the $2000 you have paid him plus an additional $500 as a penalty for not living up to the contract.

The contract in this example provides both protection for you and guarantees for Joe. The use of milestones (demonstrable steps toward completion) and progress payments assures Joe that he will have to wait until the completion of the project to see some rewards for his hard work. The penalty clauses both protect you and motivate Joe to finish the project on time. Additionally, they provide for specific remedies in case of a default.

The last area to be covered in our discussion of custom software is software performance. There are three areas of software performance to be concerned about when contracting for custom software: performance in regard to features and operational specifications, performance in regard to general usability, and assurances of future continued performance.

Performance in regard to features and operational specifications is relatively easy to determine. A program either works as detailed in the specification document or it doesn't. The data entry screens and reports either look like the samples or they don't. If the specification document states (and shows) that a menu will be used to select one of several options and the software when delivered requires a complex set of instructions (rather than the menu) to choose an option, then the software is obviously delivering reduced performance. This type of in-adequate performance is fairly straightforward and should be specifically provided for in the contract. Remedies can include money penalties or possibly having a third party correct the defect at the contractor's expense.

The second type of performance, general usability, is much more difficult to define and determine. If the program is to be used interactively, does it take 10 or 15 seconds to update each record? A situation such as this is extremely frustrating to a data entry operator and can render a program unusable.

A program that takes 5 hours to update a fairly small file would also fall short on usability performance, as would a program that used inordinate amounts of disk storage to store very little data. These types of performance problems are very difficult to anticipate in advance and provide for in the software contract. If you are able to think of areas where usability is critical, you should provide for them in the specification document.

The third area of performance is continued future performance. You would like assurance that the software will continue to operate as per specifications and that, if problems (or bugs) crop up, there is some assurance that these problems will be corrected. This gets into the area of software warranties and maintenance. In this regard it is wise to remember that a totally bug-free program doesn't exist. I have seen software where the program ran perfectly and reliably for almost four years and then "bombed out." All software producers are aware of this and most make every effort both to find as many bugs as possible before the customer gets the software and to support the customer after the sale. In the case of widely distributed software the "exterminating" process takes the form of a two-stage testing procedure, called alpha and beta testing, before the commercial product is sold. During the alpha test, the program is tested internally in the company and any bugs that crop up are corrected. The software is then subject to beta testing. In the beta tests, copies of the software are given to selected outside installations (users) in the hope that any other bugs will show up in real-world use before the paying customers get the software.

When you contract for custom software, you are paying for the privilege of serving as a beta test for the software. While manufacturers of packaged software generally disclaim all warranties except for the media, you should not permit this type of disclaimer on custom-written software. It would not be unreasonable to insist on a warranty that ran at least one full business cycle. For example, if the program will perform special functions at the end of a quarter (but not annually or semi-annually), a 4-month warranty is not unrealistic. If the software has a function that is performed once a year, then a warranty of 13 or 14 months is not unreasonable. The warranty should be spelled out in the contract as well as the procedures and obligations under the warranty. For example, your contractor may insist on written notice of a problem falling under warranty provisions, while you may insist that the contractor guarantee to fix the problem within 7 days (or 30 days, etc.) of written notification.

Having software customized or written for you can provide you with features and abilities not available in packaged software. Along with the rewards, however, it also exposes you to additional potential for problems. This potential in itself should not discourage you. Knowing where the potential for problems is will lessen the possibility that you will encounter them.

9

SPECIFIC APPLICATIONS

As mentioned previously, the availability of inexpensive computers has resulted in a plethora of software packages hitting the market. It seems as if everyone and his brother has written the definitive general ledger (or payroll, etc.). With all the software available, it is sometimes difficult to determine which features are worthwhile. This is a problem even for many people who are used to dealing with computer-generated reports. This chapter will examine some of the specific applications mentioned previously and discuss some of the things you will be coming across in your investigations.

GENERAL LEDGER

General ledger is the most popular accounting application implemented on personal computers. Packages vary greatly in price and complexity. There are several implementations of general ledger aimed at the professional accountant which offer additional features beyond those which a small business might want.

In choosing a general ledger (G/L) package to be used for client write-up work there are several things to look for. The most important quality a G/L must have is flexibility. While most G/L software will conform to "standard" bookkeeping and accounting conventions, you may need different features and capabilities of the package to meet the differing requirements of your clients. Some of your clients may require that you maintain separate cash books (disbursements, receipts, sales, etc.), while with other clients you may be able to put all entries through the general journal. Another thing to examine in evaluating G/L software is whether a set of books can easily be reopened for additional adjustments after the period has been closed. Are report formats flexible enough to suit a variety of differing business organizations? Balance sheet presentations are usually different when dealing with incorporated and un-incorporated businesses. The income statement for a retail business will usually include a "cost of goods sold" section, while that of a service organization (like your firm) will not. Will the software permit departmental reporting, multicompany reporting, and/or consolidation? Is the actual general ledger report in a format you feel comfortable with? Some clients may require a yearly G/L with all transactions shown. Many G/L packages do not archive (store) the transaction detail, but erase it when you close a period. Does the package provide all the reports you might require? If not, you will have to judge whether the missing reports are critical.

There are also some general features you should examine. These are not necessarily client-oriented items, but determine how easily your staff can use the software. The first of these items is general software usability. Is the software menu-driven? This "user-friendly" feature presents you with a "menu" of choices and allows you to select a system operation by inputting the number (or letter) of your choice. A sample menu is illustrated in Fig. 9-1.

If, at the Main Menu level, you wished to print an income statement, you would key in a "4" when asked for your selection. This would bring up the Report Menu on the screen (illustrated in Fig. 9-2). At the Report Menu you would key in a "5" ("PRINT INCOME STATEMENT"). The system would print an income statement, then redisplay the Report Menu. At this point you could print another report, or return to the Main Menu to perform another function, or exit from the G/L system.

GENERAL LEDGER MAIN MENU

CLIENT: JOE'S BAR   TODAY'S DATE: 01/06/83

PERIOD ENDING: 12/31/82

0. CHANGE CLIENT
1. CHANGE TODAY'S DATE
2. CHANGE PERIOD ENDING
3. DATA ENTRY MENU
4. REPORT GENERATION MENU
5. MAINTENANCE MENU
6. CLOSE PERIOD/YEAR
9. EXIT TO OPERATING SYSTEM
    YOUR SELECTION: _____

FIGURE 9-1 A Sample Menu

GENERAL LEDGER REPORT MENU

CLIENT: JOE'S BAR   TODAY'S DATE: 01/06/83

PERIOD ENDING: 12/31/82

1. PRINT JOURNALS
2. PRINT TRIAL BALANCE
3. PRINT GENERAL LEDGER
4. PRINT BALANCE SHEET
5. PRINT INCOME STATEMENT
6. PRINT TRIAL BALANCE WORKSHEET
9. RETURN TO MAIN MENU
    YOUR SELECTION: _____

FIGURE 9-2 A Sample Report Menu

Data entry is another area where software can be made user-friendly. One common technique is to request the G/L account number, then check to see if it is a valid account. If the amount does not exist in the chart of accounts, the operator is immediately notified. If it does exist, the account title is displayed so that the operator may verify that the entry is being made to the correct account. Many packages have another feature that eases the task of data entry, automatic offset in the cash journals. With this feature, whoever sets up the client's books on the system specifies offset accounts. As an example, the offset for disbursements would most likely be the cash-in-bank account. The operator would key in the checks, and the system would automatically make up the offsetting entry to be posted to cash.

Part of the data entry process is verification that the input is valid. This can be done in two ways. On-line verification, described above, checks the validity at the time the data are entered. This method has the benefit of instant feedback, but is much slower than accepting all the input and then checking validity. It has an additional disadvantage when you or one of your staff adds a new account for a client and forgets to bring this to the operator's attention so that the account can be added to the chart of accounts before the data entry process begins. In this situation, when the operator gets to the entry referencing the new account, he or she will encounter an "account does not exist" message and either have to exit the data entry program to add the account or post the entry to a suspense account, finish up the data entry, add the account, then go back into the data entry program to make an adjusting entry.

The second method of verification is to allow all data without verification on input. Once data entry is finished, then print an edit report detailing accounts which don't exist and unbalanced entries. The operator then calls up the incorrect transaction and corrects it. It is very important, to insure proper internal control, that the software prevent the operator from making any further changes to the transactions once they have been "finally accepted" or posted to the ledger. The system should require that any changes or corrections done after this point be done with an adjusting journal entry.

An additional time-saving feature of some G/L software is the ability to set up recurring journal entries. This feature lets you set a journal entry once and the system will automatically add the entry every operating cycle. This is used for entries for items such as depreciation or amortization which generally do not vary from period to period during the year.

Up to this point we have examined features that might be found in most G/L software produced for general purpose (that is, any small business). There are a number of packages being produced that have features that accountants would find especially useful. The most common of these is the ability to do "after-the-fact" payroll. This feature allows you, during the write-up, to enter payroll checks, distributed from gross to net, into the various balance sheet and income accounts. A subsidiary payroll ledger is also kept. Most software with this feature will produce various monthly, quarterly, and yearly reports. Some give you the option of producing various forms such as 941 schedule A (still used by some states), unemployment insurance reports, and W-2s at the end of the year.

Another feature found on many accountant-oriented G/L packages is a more extensive reporting capability. While most general-use G/L software will provide at least a journal report, trial balance, general ledger transaction report, balance sheet, and income statement, a package intended for the accounting firm will offer additional reports that the general user would not usually need. These include a "statement of changes in financial position," comparative financial statements, depreciation schedules, and notes to the financial statements. Additionally, some software can produce various transmittal letters for audit, review, or compilation engagements.

Several other features to be found on some write-up packages are the ability to do quick client setup using a "standard" chart of accounts (this eliminates having to key in the same 100 or 150 accounts every time you wish to set up a new client's books) and the ability to transfer general ledger figures at year end into a tax return preparation package.

One thing to keep in mind as you evaluate software (any software, not only G/L) is that no matter what features or "bells and whistles" the software has, if it is overly difficult to use, chances are that it will get very little use.

TIME AND BILLING

Accounts receivable is one of the more neglected areas in many small firms' practice management. The general approach of most accountants is on the line of "When was the last time we billed out Joe's Bar? That long ago! We better get out a bill to him." While your approach to billing may not be quite as casual as that, many firms have no set (or very loose) policy and procedures for this aspect of cash management. Getting bills out to the clients promptly has a benefit beyond the obvious improvement in cash flow. Haphazard billing tends to have a negative effect on a client's promptness in making payment. After all, if it took you two months to get out a bill, why should you expect a check back within two weeks?

There are two approaches to implementing an accounts receivable application in your practice. The first of these is to use standard accounts receivable (A/R) software. If your practice does not require the features to be found in more extensive "time-and-billing" packages (discussed below), this will probably be the better of the two solutions. General-purpose A/R software is usually easier to use than specialized time-and-billing software.

There are two main areas to focus on in evaluating A/R software. "User friendliness" in A/R software is extremely important. In addition to the areas of "friendliness" detailed in the discussion of general ledger software, A/R software should require a minimum of input and effort to both generate client statements and record client payments. If generating statements and recording payments are overly complex, chances are that everyone involved in the process will avoid using the new system.

Your second area of focus in evaluating the appropriateness of general-use A/R software should be on the format of the statement. Much of the available accounts receivable software is not really designed for service businesses. Many of these also require the use of a particular printed statement form for which the software has been programmed. You must evaluate the particular form or format for its appropriateness with your clients. Other features you will evaluate are the ability to generate statements on demand, recurring billings, past-due notices, and reports.

The ability to generate a statement on demand, without having to wait until the end of the month and without having to generate statements for all your clients, is an important feature. This feature is extremely useful when you are billing on completion of a service, such as for a tax audit or preparation of a tax return. As mentioned before, prompt billing encourages prompt payment. If a tax client, arriving to pick up his return, is presented with your bill at the same time as the return, chances are that he will be more prompt in his payment than if a bill arrives three or four weeks later, after he has signed and sent off the return. At the same time, while you want to be able to generate a client statement on demand, you will not want to have to print out 50 other clients' statements every time you wish a single statement.

Recurring billings is a feature that is more commonly found in time-and-billing rather than general-use A/R software. It is, however, an extremely useful function, especially to the smaller accounting firm. A great majority of the clients in smaller accounting practices are billed at a flat fee rather than on a "time-spent" basis. Depending on the client, this amount may be billed monthly, quarterly, semiannually, or annually. Software with a recurring billing feature allows you to set up a client on the system so that she is billed a set amount at a fixed, specified interval. This not only cuts down on the amount of effort needed to generate a bill, but also frees you from trying to remember who gets billed with what frequency.

The number and frequency of reports generated by A/R software vary from package to package. While it may be impressive to have the software generate 500 pages of printout each month, chances are that there are only three reports you will find consistently useful. Probably the most important report (aside from statements) that an A/R package should produce is an *aged accounts receivable trial balance*. This report lists the outstanding balance of each client and shows the age (or ages) of the balances. Many packages let you specify the aging periods. This one report shows you the firm's entire accounts receivable situation at a glance. The second useful report you will want is a *past-due report* listing only client balances which are past a specified age. The last report you will generally find useful is a *client history report*. This report details, on a client-by-client basis, all charges and payments for up to several years. Having this information in one place helps when you have to trace a payment or recall what you billed a client for a particular service or determine when his last fee increase was.

Some firms will not want to use a general-use accounts receivable package for various reasons. The statement format may be inappropriate for the firm's clients, or the general-use software may just not be flexible enough to provide the features the firm wants.

Most medium-size and large accounting firms bill on a time-spent or hourly basis. While you may not be able to charge your clients in this manner, you may still want or require the flexibility available with more specialized time-and-billing (T&B) software. The preceding discussion on accounts receivable software holds equally true for T&B software. There are several additional features in T&B software that you may find useful, but there are also several areas where potential problems may arise. Ease of data entry is one area that you should investigate more carefully than with general-use A/R software. Because T&B software has much greater flexibility in the way you can bill your clients, it generally requires greater effort on the part of everyone involved. As mentioned before, if a system is overly complex to use, it generally will be used very infrequently. This extra effort is required not only of your operator, but from most of your staff, if you want to use one of the most beneficial features of this type of software.

While greatly increased flexibility in billing methods is one major benefit of T&B software, another large benefit of this type of software is the ability to account for time spent in various tasks. This practice management function can provide you with a detailed analysis of the time spent by your staff (and yourself) on various clients and tasks, but requires that fairly extensive records be kept. These "time logs" may not only prove an annoyance to your staff, but may also provide a great amount of resentment on their part. It is important, if you decide to implement this type of software, to prepare and educate your staff. To be effective, this type of information-gathering system requires complete cooperation from your employees. You are much more likely to obtain this cooperation if they feel the information they provide will not be used against them.

Time-and-billing software also provides some benefits in the billing process. These packages usually provide great flexibility in billing methods. Most allow a mixture of methods on the same statement. These methods include "recurrent billing," time-based billing (hourly and daily), multiple-rate billing (this allows the same employee to be billed at different rates for different tasks), billing on a per job or special flat fee basis, and flexible billing for expense reimbursement.

As well as being flexible in billing methods, many T&B packages are flexible in the format of the statement. While a great majority of general-use A/R software uses preprinted, rigidly formatted forms, T&B software generally prints your statements on letterhead or plain white paper. Most T&B packages also provide some measure of control over what will appear on the statement and where on the statement it will appear. This is useful if on occasion you do not want certain details to show on the statement.

ACCOUNTS PAYABLE

Accounts payable is a fairly straightforward application in most practices. The bills come in, then several weeks later the checks go out. In selecting an A/P package there are several points to consider. The first area of consideration is the frequency and quantity of your payables. If you write only 15 or 20 checks a month, you will probably find it easier to continue doing so manually. An accounts payable package provides the greatest benefits in an environment where numerous checks are written. If you currently are writing checks many times throughout the month, you may find that a computerized A/P does not provide the flexibility you desire. Computerized A/P systems are generally run either weekly, semimonthly, or monthly. The frequency is dependent upon two factors: whether you take advantage (or wish to take advantage) of trade discounts, and the average number of transactions that accumulate in a fixed period. If you have a large dollar amount of payables subject to time-based discounts, then you will probably want to run the system, at least past the check-printing process, fairly often throughout the month. By the same token, if you normally receive a large volume of invoices, you may want to enter these at frequent intervals but print checks only once or twice a month.

If you anticipate either of these situations, make sure that the packages you are considering offer this type of flexibility. Another feature to examine is how the system handles hand-drawn checks. You will need this feature if you intend to print checks only once or twice a month and you have a weekly payroll to meet (unless you also intend to install a payroll system). Some systems handle hand checks with less bother than others. There are also internal control considerations. Accounts payable is an application that is very sensitive to poor control. Internal control can be implemented and maintained through a number of methods. Varying levels of passwords should be required to access different levels of A/P functions. Purchase journals or vouchers can be used. Specific authorization for all payments should be required, and the system should maintain easily traced audit trails. Changes to inputted data should be allowed only by a method that leaves a visible, obvious audit trail. Checks should be prenumbered, with physical access to them restricted. A check log (detailing range of check numbers used in a run as well as voided checks) and a check register should both be maintained. Any voided checks should be marked "void" and stapled into the check log, not destroyed.

The reports generated by the A/P system serve two functions. There is the obvious one of cash management. This function is served by reports such as a "cash requirements schedule" (which shows the cash needed if all payments are to be made through a specified due date); a "due-date register," which lists payables in order by their due dates with their terms (this is used to take advantage of net terms or to defer paying large payables until they are due, giving you longer use of your cash); and an "A/P aging report" (detailing how much of your payables is current, and what, if any, is past due).

The other function some A/P reports serve is control. The check authorization report (or check request report) and the check register are both an important part of the audit trail. The check authorization (or request) report lists outstanding payables, their terms, age, and amount. This report is examined by the person responsible for authorizing payment who determines whether or not an invoice gets paid in the near future. On those items he wants paid, he marks a pay date and his initials. This document then serves as the source document for the operator to input which invoices to pay and is saved for audit purposes. After the checks are printed, a check register is run and is stored with previous check registers.

One final consideration on accounts payable software is whether or not special checks are needed. Many software packages use "standard" continuous checks available at reasonable prices from business forms suppliers like NEBS or Checks-to-Go. Some suppliers of software, however, require specially laid-out checks available only from them at unreasonable prices.

PAYROLL

Payroll is an unusual application inasmuch as it may be easier to remain on a manual system if your payroll is a small one or to use an outside service bureau if your payroll is a large one. This is because payroll is a "labor-intensive" application. Payroll requires a great deal of human attention both to process and to maintain, whether it is a manual or computerized system. Time-consuming verification is needed in several places in a "standard" microcomputer-based payroll system. Additionally, the maintenance functions involved in both payroll changes or corrections and employee file maintenance also require an inordinate amount of time. I have generally found payroll a feasible application on personal computers only within a range of from about 15 to about 30 or 40 employees.

The major benefits a computerized payroll offers the small firm are the ability to make a timely determination of payroll tax deposit requirements and having payroll information easily at hand at quarter and year end. These benefits can also be realized by using a write-up system with "after-the-fact" payroll capability or throwing together a similar recordkeeping system with one of the data-base system packages.

If an in-house payroll is implemented on your system, internal control considerations and solutions are similar to those discussed under accounts payable.

Most small practices have many more word processing tasks than might first be obvious. Besides letters and memos to clients, there are reports to be typed, numerous letters to various governmental agencies, and various other typing tasks. While word processing will not totally replace your typewriter (there are times when it does not make sense to use a word processor), it can simplify many common typing tasks in your practice, as well as being useful for client development.

Word processing becomes even more attractive when you consider that it's almost a "freebie." Your initial investment in personal computer hardware and software to perform write-up and other tasks in your office may run to about $3000 or more. For an additional $300 or $400 you can turn this equipment into a full-feature word processor equal to dedicated word processing equipment that sells for $8000 or more. In examining word processing software, there are several things to look at. The first item to determine is ease of use. The more features word processing software has, generally the more difficult it is to use. While complexity of use is not necessarily a disadvantage in itself, poor documentation can render the software useless. Many of the more complex word processors provide special keyboard layouts such as mnemonics (where the function of a key is tied into the letter on the key). An example of this is using the "control" key and the "E" to erase a letter. Other producers supply keytop overlays. These are adhesive pieces of plastic that have the various commands printed on them and stick to the tops of the keys. This eliminates many trips back to the manual once some familiarity with the software has been achieved. Another helpful item of many packages is a reference card detailing the various commands and their uses.

Your choice of word processing software will depend on several factors, including the particular hardware you have picked out, but your most important consideration should be what you intend to do with it. If your intended use involves complex manipulation, such as moving blocks of text around, then you will want to consider one of the more "full-feature" packages. If your needs are simple, you will probably be better off with software that is easier to learn and use.

As mentioned before, there are some circumstances where word processors are less efficient than your old standby, the typewriter. Word processing excels in repetitive typing tasks—form letters, standard reports, client memos and instruction sheets, and the like. In these applications you store the body of the document, then, when needed, plug in the information that is specific to the particular occasion. Tasks such as short, one-time memos are probably still easier to do on a typewriter.

Some of the uses for word processing, including form letters personalized with your clients' names, have been detailed earlier. Another practice development aid is the client newsletter. Preparation of newsletters and bulletins is a much simpler task using a word processor than a typewriter.

Considering the cost/benefit ratio inherent in software for word processing, you can hardly go wrong whichever package you select.

TAX RETURN PREPARATION AND MODELING

Just as using a service bureau for preparation of tax returns provides many benefits over doing them by hand, preparing tax returns on your in-house computer has benefits over doing them with a service bureau. The most obvious benefit of in-house preparation is that it is very inexpensive compared with service bureaus. Most service bureaus charge between $10 and $20 a return, depending on complexity and whether state or local returns are required. Taking $15 as an average processing cost per return, processing 100 returns per tax season will cost $1500 per year. Over a period of 3 years, the cost will be $4500, which is probably as much or more than you spent on your entire computer. While tax return preparation software is fairly expensive to buy initially (prices range from several hundred to several thousand dollars), once the initial purchase has been made, updates for following years are usually very inexpensive. If a package has an initial cost of $1000 and updates for the next 2 years run $400 a year, then after 3 years you have saved $2700 over having a service bureau do them. Even if you add in labor costs of having someone key in the information, at $3 a return (½ hour at $6 per hour) for 300 returns (100/year × 3 years), you still have a savings of $1800.

This reduction in costs, while one of the more obvious benefits of doing returns in-house, is probably not the one you will appreciate the most. The one area in which most, if not all, service bureaus fall down is on turnaround time. If your service bureau offers courier service (and if you decide to spring for the additional expense), it will still take at least a day for your return to get to the bureau and an additional day to be returned to you. Add 2 days for processing and collating and the best turnaround you could expect would be 4 days. When things start to become busy, most likely this will slip to 5 or 6 days. If you use the U.S. mail rather than a courier, a turnaround of 7 to 10 days is not unlikely. If (heaven forbid) an error has been made in keying in the return, or you have entered a wrong figure, another week goes by.

With your own system you can have almost instant turnaround if you need it. On those returns where there is less urgency, you will probably want to process several returns at once, perhaps once a day or every other day. Most tax return software gives you the option of using it in an interactive mode or batch mode. Using the software in an interactive mode lets you input the information and see the results immediately. You can then either print the return or defer printing until a later time. Using the software in batch mode requires that all information for one or more returns be entered. At a later time, several returns are printed one after the other. Using the software in an interactive mode gives you the results immediately, while batch mode makes more effective use of time.

Tax modeling is another excellent use for personal computing equipment. This application can be implemented either with specialized modeling software or by using a return preparation package in an interactive mode. Modeling allows you to enter your estimates of a client's income and deductions and then, by changing the figures, quickly determine the tax effects of different strategies. Thus you can quickly determine the effect of deferring particular items of income and/or deductions. All return preparation software that can be used in an interactive mode can be used this way. Batch-mode-only software can, of course, be used for this purpose also, although the time lag between trying a strategy and seeing its effect can be frustrating.

The advantage to using software specifically designed for modeling is that it allows you to spread the model over several years. Some modeling software allows you to build models of between 5 and 10 years. This permits you to see the overall effect of strategies such as income averaging and using the special 10-year method on lump sum distributions.

Tax return preparation and tax modeling are excellent applications for microcomputers. In many cases the benefits from these two applications alone can justify the purchase of an entire system.

10

ADVANCED APPLICATIONS FOR MICROCOMPUTERS

Once you've acquired your in-house system and had a chance to use it for a while, you will find yourself looking for more and more ways your computer can be useful in the firm. The applications discussed in this chapter are not for rank beginners but will give you some ideas to pursue once you have become comfortable with the new electronic staff member in your office.

COMPUTER LANGUAGES, PROGRAM GENERATORS, AND DATA BASE SOFTWARE

After you have had a chance to get used to your computer you will probably start coming up with new ways to use it. Some of these applications will be available as off-the-shelf packages. Others, however, you will have to write yourself or have written for you. Computer programming, while not necessarily difficult, is beyond the scope of this book. What we will discuss are the various methods of producing custom applications.

Computer languages can be broadly divided into two general types, procedural and nonprocedural languages, which,

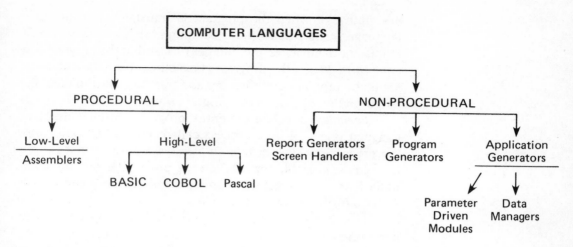

FIGURE 10-1 Language Families

in turn, are further subdivided (see Fig. 10-1). *Procedural languages* are those whose instructions are concerned with each tiny step in the process of manipulating data. They consist of "high-level" and "low-level" languages. *Low-level languages*, such as *assemblers*, are closely related in structure to the actual machine language the computer uses. They are usually more efficient (than high-level languages) at using the computer's resources, but are much more difficult for an inexperienced user to program in.

High-level languages are oriented more toward human use. While assemblers use mnemonics to represent machine language commands, high-level languages use words such as "read" and "write" as well as arithmetic operations such as "+" and "−" to perform data moving and manipulation. There are many computer languages available, each having many proponents and detractors. Common languages available on micro-based systems include BASIC, COBOL, FORTRAN, Pascal, APL, C, and PL/1. Most applications run on personal computers today have been written in one of the varieties of BASIC, although Pascal is beginning to gain in popularity. High-level languages come in one or more of three basic forms: interpreters, compilers, and pseudocompilers. Any computer language, whether high-level or low-level, must be translated into machine language before the computer can execute it. The three "forms" listed above are descriptive of when the program is translated into machine language. *Interpreters* store the computer program in *source code*, that is, the same letter and number format that the program was entered in. When the program is executed (run), the computer loads the program into memory and translates it into machine language line by line as the program runs.

Compilers translate the entire program into machine language at one time (in a process called "compiling") and store the program on disk or tape in *object code* format, that is, in a machine-executable form. When the program is run, the computer loads the object code program into memory and runs it with no further processing needed.

Pseudocompilers compile the source code program into an *intermediate code* format. When the program is run, this intermediate code is translated, line by line, into machine, or object, code which the computer executes.

Each form (interpreter, compiler, and pseudocompiler) has its advantages and disadvantages. An interpreter is the easiest to use from a development standpoint, as most interpreters will point out errors in syntax (usage) at the time the program is entered. Compilers require that the program be entered with an editor program, compiled, any errors corrected with the editor, then recompiled. This is a lengthy process. The major advantage of a compiler is that programs written with one generally run much faster than programs written with an interpreter. Compiled programs usually take up more storage space than interpreted ones. Pseudocompilers, such as CBASIC, try to compromise. They run faster than interpreted versions of the language (but slower than compiled versions), but take up more storage space than an interpreted version (although less than a compiled version of the language).

In most cases, a relative newcomer to programming will be best off using an interpreted version of a language. It will be a much less frustrating experience, and the feedback generated by the interpreter's refusing to accept an instruction with the wrong syntax will prove educational.

Perhaps a better choice for the novice would be a *nonprocedural language*. Most of these so-called languages are not languages at all, but systems to perform data processing tasks. While languages like BASIC are concerned with the "nuts and bolts" of processing data (read a record, multiply one piece of information by another, write the record back onto the disk), nonprocedural "languages" tend to be more concerned with the application than with the mechanics of what the computer has to go through to process data. Nonprocedural languages can be broadly grouped into three general divisions: report generators, program generators, and application generators.

While nonprocedural languages are being touted as the "fourth-generation languages of the 1980s," *report generators* have been around, in one form or the other, since the early 1960s. RPG (Report Program Generator) has been offered by several of the mainframe manufacturers since the second computer generation (these were the transistorized machines) and has been available in various incarnations (RPGII and RPGIII) ever since. While RPG in its various forms has been considered a programmable language, it has its own, internal logic and must be used with that internal logic in mind. The application is developed by describing it on several different varieties of forms. There is no need to write programs in computer code to accept input from a keyboard or punched cards and put the information into a disk file. Instead, the "programmer" describes what the input to the application system should be and what data should be stored on the various disk files. She then fills out forms describing what (if any) computations are to be made and the format of any reports desired. The RPG compiler takes these specifications and generates the code (instructions) the computer requires to accomplish all these tasks.

While the RPG language is not widely available for personal computers, there are several software packages, when used together, that provide a similar facility. Packages called *screen handlers* take care of the data entry tasks. This software, such as MicroPro's DATASTAR, Fox and Geller's QUICKSCREEN, and STATCOM's CRTform allow the user to specify what input is expected and what range of values is acceptable for each input item. The package then provides the data entry screens for the CRT and builds a desk file containing the entered data. Many of these packages allow the user to specify that new data fields be created from the mathematical manipulation of entered data. When this type of software is used with a report generation package such as Friends Software's ACCESS/80, which will generate almost any type of report from a user's description, then functional equivalence to an RPG-type language has been achieved.

Additional development tools can be found in program generators and applications generators. *Program generators* work similarly to RPG languages. Information about the application, such as what information the data files will contain, report formats, and so on, is keyed into the program generator. This information is then used by the software to generate actual computer programs to do data entry, file maintenance, print reports, and so forth. These generated programs are in source code in various languages, and can be modified by a programmer. Program generators vary in their ability to handle complex applications such as multifile access and in the amount of the application generated. Some, such as Fox and Geller's QUICKSCREEN and STATCOM's CRTform, are primarily screen handlers (generate programs to do data entry), while others such as Relational System's PEARL and Software Group's PROGRAMMER'S APPRENTICE generate entire applications systems. Relational System's PEARL generates programs in a version of BASIC called CBASIC 2, while PROGRAMMER'S APPRENTICE generates code in Microsoft BASIC (BASIC-80). There is even a program generator, Marramoty and Scotto Software's C.O.R.P., that generates programs in Apple Computers' own version of BASIC, APPLESOFT.

Similar in function to program generators, but not generating computer language code, are *application generators*. These consist of two general types: parameter-driven modules and data managers. Both of these work in much the same way, although most *data base management systems* on personal computers are limited as to the complexity of the applications that can be generated with them. So-called data base managers on microcomputers allow the user to input data to a disk file and print simple reports from the information.

Parameter-driven development systems, as well as most true data base managers, allow the developer to specify application system information in much the same manner as program generators. This information is stored as a file on one of the disk units. When a user wants to enter data, a data entry program module looks at the specification file to see what input is expected, then formats the CRT screen to present a "custom" data entry screen to the user. To print a report, the same general logic is followed. A generalized report-printing program looks at the specification file to see what the designer has specified for the particular report the user has requested, then uses those "parameters" to print a specific report. Some examples of this type of software include Personal PEARL from Relational Systems, Configurable Business System and FORMULA from Dynamic Microprocessor Associates, and MBDS from ISE. The major difference between application generators and data base management systems is the manner in which they store data. Program and application generators store information in data files (think of a file as a drawer in a filing cabinet). Each type of data is usually stored in a separate file. For example, a client's chart of accounts would be stored in one file, while current transactions would be stored in another file. At the end of the period, the transaction file would be used to update the balances in the chart-of-accounts file, then deleted or archived in a history file. Data base managers generally use only one file, called a data base, to store differing types of information. The relationships of one piece of information to another, as well as the "parameters" needed for reports and data entry, are stored in a separate file called the *data dictionary*. Some data base systems have separate languages to define the format of the data base (called *data definition languages*) and to retrieve data from the data base (called *data query languages*). Two additional terms you will often run into in data base literature are *relational* and *hierarchal*. These terms are used to denote the relationship between individual pieces of information and how the data base is accessed. The actual theory behind data base systems is somewhat beyond the scope of this book and the casual user. Relational data base systems have gained great popularity in recent years, and most true data base software available for personal computers seems to be based on this type of organization.

WHEN TO USE WHAT

The particular type of development software you will choose will, of course, be largely dependent on what you need to accomplish. For most simple, single-file (or two-file) applications such as mailing lists and the like, you will most likely want to use a screen handler/report generator combination or an application generator. Program generators usually offer no advantages with this type of application. If the application you are developing requires the use and maintenance of multiple files or requires features beyond those offered by application generators, you will probably want to use a program generator to produce much of the system, with the remainder to be coded by a programmer. True data base managers are used to develop complex applications in which different applications use information contained in one data base.

Development software will allow a relatively unsophisticated computer user to generate entire application systems in a very short period of time and with much less effort than programming by hand. The fly in the ointment is that none of these development aids lessens the need for thinking the system through. If the system has been poorly designed, an application (or program) generator will very rapidly generate a poor application system. Perhaps the greatest boon to using these tools is that your errors in design are uncovered fairly quickly.

FORECASTING AND "ELECTRONIC SPREADSHEETS"

One of the banes of every accountant's life is the spreadsheet. Every accountant has had the experience of sitting down with an analysis pad, ruler, and calculator to make up schedules, pro formas, and cash budgets. Most accountants don't enjoy doing this very much. Neither did Dan Bricklin who, as a graduate business student several years ago, decided to do something about it. Together with his friend Bob Frankston, he came up with a spreadsheet simulator for the Apple Computer. The success story of VisiCalc has become a legend in the computing industry. Originally available only for the Apple, it is now available for many other systems. For CP/M-based systems where VisiCalc may not be available, several other software producers have brought out their versions of spreadsheet simulators.

Software such as Sorcim's SuperCalc, Micropro's CalcStar, and Chang Laboratories' MicroPlan appear and are used very much like VisiCalc.

These "electronic spreadsheets" have two very powerful attributes. The first is the ability to define mathematical relationships between any of the *cells* (a cell is the intersection of a row and a column). When relationships have been defined, changing the figure in one cell will update the other cells for which the relationship has been defined. This recalculation ability can be used to good advantage in forecasting, budgeting, and pro forma modeling ("Now . . . if I change this figure, what will happen to the bottom line?"). The second feature that gives these programs tremendous power and usability is their built-in functions. These include trigonometric functions (such as sine, cosine, etc.), logical functions such as true and false, various arithmetic functions (such as average, sum, log), and present-value functions. These allow the construction of very complex models as well as making the construction of depreciation schedules and amortization tables very simple.

If your models tend to be very complex, there are software packages for personal computers specifically designed for modeling. These packages, sometimes referred to as *decision support systems* (DSS), differ from the electronic spread-sheets in several ways. As they are specifically designed with modeling in mind, complex models are easier to construct (though simpler models may take longer than if you used a spread-sheet simulator). Modeling software generally has extended built-in functions, including many statistical functions. These statistical functions can range from standard deviation to multiple linear regression (curve-fitting). Some software such as MICRO DSS/FINANCE by Addison-Wesley and MICRO-FINESSE by Osborne/McGraw-Hill have extensive graphics capability (such as color pie charts, etc.), while others such as Visicorp's DESKTOP-PLANII and Comshare's TARGET are slightly more limited in their graphic presentation of data.

Spreadsheet simulators are excellent applications for implementation on personal computers. The novice user can use them for schedules and pro formas, then, as experience and confidence are gained, continue on with them to progressively more sophisticated uses.

TELECOMMUNICATIONS

Most accountants gain an appreciation for the value of information. They have been taught that accounting systems are information gathering and management systems. Managerial (cost) accounting and finance courses emphasize that in the decision-making process, information has value. Accountants talk about the cost of "more perfect" information. This book has already discussed the role of personal computers in providing both you and your clients with more timely (and thus more valuable) information. In addition to this, your microcomputer can provide you with the means to access vast *information resources*—companies that maintain vast amounts of data on various subjects in data bases on large computer systems. Access to these data bases is provided by connecting a terminal to the various systems over the regular dial phone network.

There are several suppliers of this type of information resource, each providing some services that are unique and some which overlap with services offered by others. In all cases your computer can be used as a terminal (more on this later).

Perhaps the largest selection of data bases available to the "average user" is provided by Lockheed's DIALOG service. DIALOG currently boasts well over 150 different data bases (with more added each month) covering diverse subjects such as medicine, economics, and so on. These data bases can be searched and references and abstracts can be printed at your terminal or off-line and sent to you. Data bases of interest to accountants include Standard & Poor's reports, the *Congressional Record*, information from Dun & Bradstreet, and 10K information filed with the SEC. To use DIALOG you must request a password from Lockheed. At present there is no charge for a password nor minimum monthly billing. You are charged for your searches based on the time used while the computer is searching. While the costs vary from $60 up to $150 an hour (depending on the particular data base you are using), most searches, if they are thought out before you connect to DIALOG, take only several minutes and cost very little.

An additional information resource of particular interest to the accountant is the AICPA's time-sharing library. This library, containing programs used for tax modeling and planning as well as programs for help with audit chores, is maintained by the AICPA on TYMSHARE'S time-sharing computer network.

In many cases, commercially available software running on your microcomputer will do the job just as well (if not better). If you feel that your needs will not be adequately met using your micro in this area, you might want to look at this time-sharing library. More information can be obtained from the AICPA or TYMSHARE. (You must be an AICPA member to access the library.)

In addition to the large commercial data base suppliers, there are two information resources available to you at very little cost. These are The Source (a division of Reader's Digest Corporation) and Micro-Net (provided by Compuserve, a division of H&R Block). Both these services provide inexpensive access to information on a great deal of subjects. At present the charge for both services is between $5 and $10 an hour after business hours (after 6:00 P.M.). Both services have stock prices, programs for financial calculations, and lots of other information. If you are having problems with your software or equipment, you can put a message on an "electronic bulletin board" and, in many cases, get answers from all over the world. Both services offer "electronic mail" where you can send an electronic letter to another subscriber almost instantaneously.

If you decide to use these information resources, there are several things that you will require. The first of these is a computer terminal. Your personal computer, coupled with a communications software program, makes an excellent terminal. There are many excellent, inexpensive software packages available that turn your computer into a "superintelligent" terminal for use with one of the telecommunications utilities mentioned above. These packages, such as Southwestern Data Systems' ASCII EXPRESS and Z-TERM, Visicorp's Visiterm, and Link Systems' DATALINK, turn the APPLE into a terminal capable of up- and downloading files to (and from) other computers. For machines running the CP/M operating system there are also many excellent packages, including Hawkeye Graphics'

COMMX, Dynamic Microprocessor Associates' ASCOM, Super-softs' TERMII, and many others. New programs come out frequently, and most are inexpensive and easy to use. (There are also many excellent programs available for the Radio Shack, Atari, Commodore, and virtually every other microcomputer on the market.)

Once you have chosen your "terminal" software, there is one other item you will need to go "on-line." This is a device called a *modem* (modulator/demodulator), which converts the information coming out of your computer into sound to be carried by the telephone network to the remote computer and converts the sound from the remote computer into information your computer can understand. This is necessary because the telephone network is capable of handling frequencies only that fall within our range of hearing.

There are two types of modems being sold for use with personal computers. One is the acoustically coupled modem. With this type of modem, the computer is linked with the phone system by placing the telephone handset into a set of foam "muffins" on the modem. The signal from your computer is converted into sound and a small speaker in the modem plays this sound into the phone handset's microphone. Information from the remote computer comes out of the handset's receiver (earpiece) and is picked up by a microphone in the modem. Acoustically coupled modems are relatively inexpensive and have been very popular in the past, but are susceptible to ambient noise and do not transmit or receive information reliably at rates greater than 300 baud (about 30 characters/second). The second type of modem is the direct-connect modem. This device connects with the telephone system by means of a modular plug which plugs into a telephone company–supplied jack (this is the same jack that a plug-in telephone uses). Direct-connect modems are not affected by room noise, and if equipped for high-speed operation, provide much more reliability at speeds up to 1200 baud (about 120 characters/second).

One additional point in favor of the direct-connect modem is that many models, such as the Hayes' MICRO-MODEM II, SMARTMODEM, Novation's APPLECAT, and others, offer options such as automatic dialing of numbers and can be programmed to automatically answer if you set up your system to provide remote access to it.

As mentioned previously, there are two major approaches to implementing a multiuser microcomputer system. The first of these, time-sharing, has been discussed in some detail earlier.

FIGURE 10-2 STAR Network

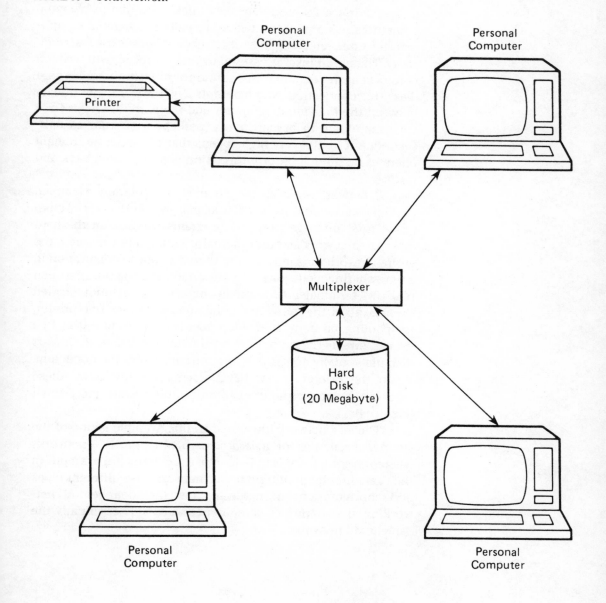

The second method, which is becoming very popular, is *networking*. Networking is a technique where several computers are configured to share common resources. These shared resources can include mass storage devices such as disk drives, printers, and telecommunications hardware. There are many methods used to configure networks. A simple method, the *star network*, is illustrated in Fig. 10-2. This simple example consists of four separate personal computers, each with its own floppy disk, sharing a 20-megabyte hard disk. One of the personal computers has a printer attached to it. The individual computers are connected together through a device called a *multiplexer*. The multiplexer is essentially an electronic switch which connects each computer, in a round-robin fashion, to the hard disk. This connection, which permits a two-way transfer of data between the individual computer and the hard disk, lasts for a very short time in human terms (perhaps a quarter- to half-second) but, at the very high speeds that computer equipment operates at, quite a bit of information can be passed back and forth.

A network such as the simple configuration exampled here allows several users, each at his own work station computer, to share large files and programs residing on the hard disk. As each work station is actually a complete computer, the entire network runs much faster than a similar configuration in a time-sharing mode (one microcomputer sharing time between four CRT terminals). Additionally, by use of a technique called *spooling*, all of the individual computers can share one printer. In spooling, an individual computer, instead of outputting to a printer, directs the output file on the hard disk (Fig. 10-3). This disk file actually contains a "picture" of the printed document. When the printer is not being used for other tasks, these "spooled" print files are transferred to this system and printed (Fig. 10-4).

The star network illustrated in this example is one of the simplest examples of a *local area network* (LAN)—networks where the equipment is in fairly close proximity (for example, in the same building). Other types of networks use different types and configurations of hardware, but the idea behind networking, the sharing of computer resources, is essentially the same in all networks.

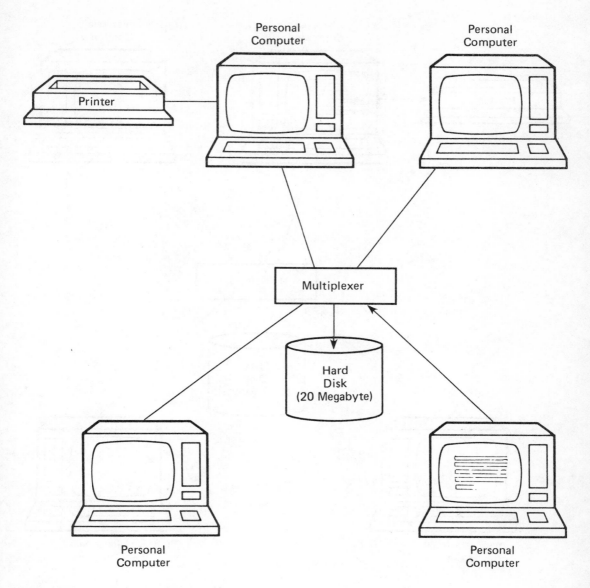

FIGURE 10-3 Spooling: Output to Disk File

GRAPHICS

As the saying goes, "A picture is worth a thousand words." Accountants, in their efforts to be precise, have largely ignored graphics in favor of the more familiar tabular formats such as

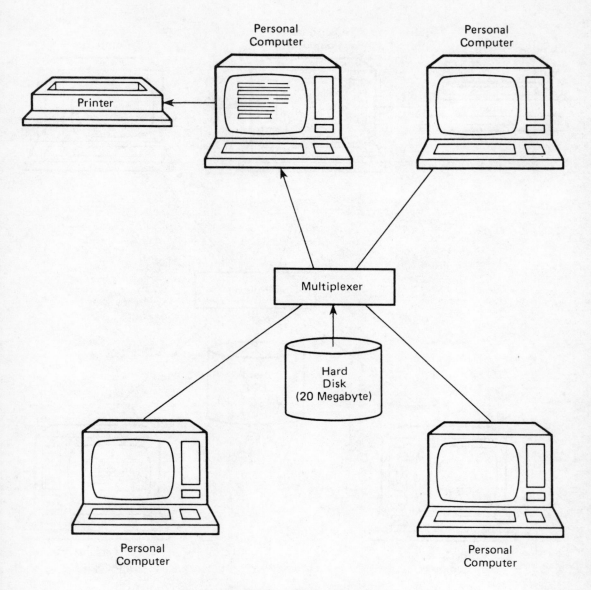

FIGURE 10-4 Spooling: File Is Sent to Printer

the balance sheet and income statement. A major purpose of these financial reports is to convey information. Unfortunately, tabular rows of numbers, while a precise method of presentation, do not always convey the information they contain in a readily understandable form. As an example of this, compare the "old-fashioned" watch with hands on a circular dial to a digital readout watch. Both of these easily convey the fact that it is 11:50 A.M. The old-style watch, however, immediately conveys that it is 10 minutes till lunch, while the digital display requires a bit of thinking about. It is for the same reason that recent accounting literature has been promoting the use of graphical presentation of financial data as a supplement to the standard tabular formats now being used.

Figure 10-5 shows a simplified Balance Sheet presented in a pie chart format. After the chart is examined for a few

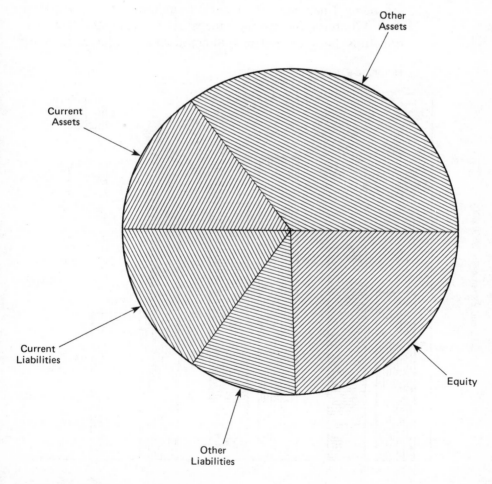

FIGURE 10-5 Pie Chart

moments, several things become immediately apparent. It is visually obvious that Current Assets and Current Liabilities are about the same size. This tells us, without much thought, that the "Current Ratio" is about 1. It is also apparent from a quick examination that, of all other assets, "Other" Assets is twice as much as Current Assets. Depending on the type of business this chart represents, it might mean the company is overcapitalized or has an excess capital investment. Also apparent on quick inspection is that Current Liabilities are almost twice the amount of "Other" Liabilities. This might indicate (again, depending on the type of business) that growth and operations are being financed out of short-term rather than long-term debt. Whatever the circumstances of this company, the relationships between Balance Sheet divisions are made more

FIGURE 10-6 Histogram

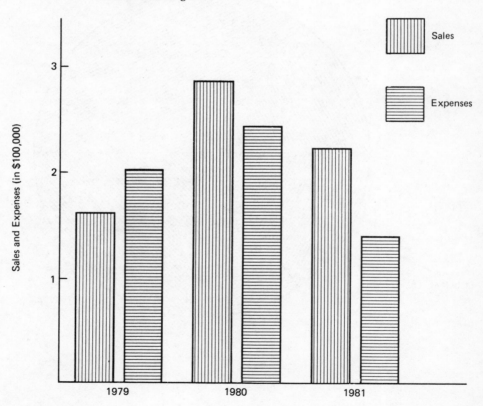

apparent with the graphical presentation. A simplified graphic presentation of a three-year comparative Income Statement is illustrated in Fig. 10-6. Again, certain things are obvious upon quick visual examination. It is readily apparent that there was a loss in 1979 (sales are exceeded by expenses) and profits in 1980 and 1981. Also obvious are the facts that sales almost doubled in 1980 over 1979 and then receded in 1981. The histogram also easily shows that of the three years presented, 1981 shows the largest profit, primarily because expenses have been substantially reduced from the prior two years. While much detail is lost in this mode of presentation, the histogram illustration of the comparative Income Statement, as in the pie chart presentation of the Balance Sheet, quickly points out the relationship of sales to expenses over the three-year period.

Much of the graphics software available for personal computers is aimed at specific hardware such as the Apple and Atari, which have extensive, built-in graphics capability. As business use of graphics increases, no doubt many similar packages will become available in machine-independent form.

AUDITING WITH A PERSONAL COMPUTER

One area of accounting where personal computers have not been extensively used is auditing. One of the major reasons for this is that audit software, as such, is available only for large minicomputers and mainframes. Additionally, this software is so expensive that only very large firms or those with extensive audit practices can justify its purchase. While many of the larger accounting firms are investigating the use of micro-computers for audit use, it is possible for the smaller practi-tioner, with a little savvy, to use readily available software on his personal computer to emulate many of the functions of expensive audit software packages. To see how this is done, we must first examine the capabilities and use of the large-system audit software packages. These packages generally have three major capabilities:

1. *Statistical.* The statistical functions of audit software fall into three categories. The first of these is to calculate sample parameters. The population size, precision, and confidence level required are fed in and the software will calculate the required sample size. Once the required sample size has been calculated, the second function, selecting the sample, takes place. The audit software uses a random-number generator to generate the item numbers to be selected. If the client's records are in a machine-readable form, the software may actually select the sample, generating a "sample file" based on the list generated by the random-number generator. The auditor then examines the sample (though some audit software will "examine" the selected items, comparing them against parameters entered by the auditor). The third statistical function the software performs is the statistical evaluation of the findings.

2. *Simulation.* The second major use of audit software is to simulate the client's software (if the client has her own computer). This is accomplished by the auditor filling out specification sheets that define the processes taking place in the client's data processing systems. Once this emulation is completed, the auditor can "walk through" transactions to see that they are being properly handled. This process is similar to the tagging of records and auditing through the client's computer.

3. *Generation of Test Data.* The third major function of audit software is the generation of "dummy" records and files. These are used by the auditor for tests on the client's computer. This can take the form of "tagged" records for use with the *integrated test facility* (ITF) method or the creation of a "test deck" if that is the method used to validate the client's system.

One additional feature of most audit packages, though not a major use, is the ability to compare a "current" copy of a client's program to an archival copy in the auditor's possession. This feature is used to verify the "purity" of the client's software.

Many of these functions can be emulated on personal computers. The statistical features of calculating sample size, choosing the sample (generating the item selection list with a random-number generator), and evaluating the results are

available in several software packages. Two of these are A-STAT
79 by Rosen Grandon Associates, which runs on the Apple II,
and MICROSTAT, a CP/M-based program distributed by Lifeboat Associates. The ability to read a data file and select records
according to specified parameters can be found in several
packages such as ACCESS/80 Level II by Friends Software and
SUPERSORT I by MicroPro. This is useful not only to select
sample records using an item list generated by a random-
number generator, but also to check a data file for the existence
of duplicate records.

Another feature of the expensive audit packages which
can be emulated is source code and core image (compiled code)
comparisons with packages such as ZAP 80 from Lifeboat
Associates, which runs under the CP/M operating system. Other
packages with similar capabilities are available for machine-
dependent operating systems.

Individual records, data files, and programs both in source
and object (compiled) formats can be transmitted from the
client's system to your system (if you are both running under
the same operating system). This is accomplished by use of
"intelligent terminal" software, modems, and the regular telephone system. Telecommunications has been discussed earlier
in this chapter. Most terminal software packages also offer
extensive data-moving capabilities. Most of these software
packages allow you to transfer not only data files and records,
but also programs. You will find this feature especially useful in
performing source and object code verifications.

Audit software packages used by larger accounting firms
have one additional major feature that can be emulated on
microcomputer systems. This is the ability to simulate a client's
application system (or part of an application system). On large-
system packages, this is accomplished by use of a nonprocedural language which is part of the audit software package.
The auditor fills out input sheets which specify the data record
formats and the computational procedures to be performed on
those records. With the large number of nonprocedural languages available on personal computers, this feature is easily
emulated. Most program and applications generators require
input similar in form and content to that required with mini-
and mainframe-based audit software.

PROJECT SCHEDULING

An area where a personal computer can be of enormous use but is often overlooked is for project scheduling and control. The methodologies of *PERT* (Program Evaluation and Review Technique) and *CPM* (Critical Path Method) were originally developed for hastening research and development and construction projects. Both PERT and CPM provide techniques for breaking down a complex project into its component tasks. After this is done, the tasks are analyzed in terms of the order they must be performed in and the time each requires. Task interdependency (which tasks must be completed before a following task can be started) is also determined. The critical path tells you which tasks are time-critical, that is, which tasks must be completed in the time estimated in order to complete the project in the least possible time. The critical path also allows the manager of the project to determine the effect of slippage (a task taking longer than estimated) upon the completion of the entire project.

While the above description does sound more appropriate to a company developing missiles or building houses, there are a couple of areas in an accounting practice where these techniques can be used to good effect. One "project" in an accounting firm that can easily be broken down into its component tasks is an audit. There are many tasks involved in conducting an audit: conducting the review of the internal control, sampling, verification of accounts, and so on. Each of these tasks consists of readily discernible subtasks. The more involved a particular audit, the more sense it makes to use project control techniques to manage it.

Project control techniques and software can be used for "projects" other than audits. Most practitioners, whether in a large or small practice, have had clients engage them for so-called special projects. These can vary from putting together financing packages to bringing a company public. All these are candidates for project management. In fact, any job that consists of time-dependent subtasks will probably benefit from the use of PERT or CPM.

In the discussion so far, we have not differentiated between PERT and CPM. In actual use, the two systems are very similar. PERT is an extension of CPM techniques. CPM is used when the time duration of the individual tasks is known or can be estimated to a fairly close degree. With projects that contain tasks whose time duration cannot be closely estimated, PERT uses built-in simulation techniques to estimate the most likely duration when given "optimistic" and "pessimistic" times.

Prior to the ready availability of personal computers, these project management techniques were only available through expensive and complex software packages or by using laborious hand diagraming and calculation methods. In 1980 a company called Organic Software introduced a project management software package called MILESTONE. This package (which is also licensed to VISICORP, which markets it as VISI-SCHEDULE for the Apple) as well as several other packages which have become available since MILESTONE's introduction are not only relatively inexpensive (most retail for less than $500), but are easy to learn and use.

If the use of project management software saves one or two days of your time or your staff's time, it has already paid for itself. Any time saved beyond that means less expense (and hopefully more profit) for your firm.

SOME LAST THOUGHTS

This book has covered a wide range of topics regarding the acquisition and use of personal computers by the accountant. At the same time, we have barely scratched the surface. The power and versatility of these little machines is such that new ways of using them come to light every day. There are many excellent software packages available which will allow you to be "up and running" with your system almost immediately. Once you have gained some confidence and facility with the system, you can utilize the many languages, development tools, and utilities to start implementing your ideas.

GLOSSARY

Alphanumeric. Text that contains (or can contain) letters, numbers, and special symbols (such as $, ×, &).

ALU (arithmetic/logical unit). The part of the central processing unit (CPU) that performs arithmetic functions (addition, subtraction, etc.) and logical comparisons.

Analog Computer. A computer that uses physical effects such as voltage or resistance to represent numeric quantities.

Assembly Language. A computer language that uses English mnemonics to represent actual machine-level operations. For example, a machine instruction to compare two quantities and, if they are equal, execute a different set of instructions ("branch if equal") might be represented as the assembler instruction BE. These instructions are converted by a translator called an assembler into machine language that can be executed by the computer.

Baud. A measurement of serial data transmission speed. In most cases, dividing the baud rate by 10 will give you the approximate rate in characters per second (e.g., 300 baud is approximately 30 characters per second).

Binary. Having two states of being. Used in computers to represent on–off.

Bit. Binary digit (0 or 1). The smallest unit of information used in a computer.

Bootstrap (or boot/booting). The process that the computer uses, on being powered up, to load the operating system.

Bug. A problem in either the computer hardware or software.

Byte. The unit the computer uses to represent a single character.

Chip. An electronic component that contains the equivalent of thousands of discrete components such as transistors, resistors, and capacitors.

COBOL (COmmon Business Oriented Language). A high-level (English-like) language which has features oriented toward its use in programming business applications (as opposed to math- or engineering-oriented languages).

Compiler. A program which translates a high-level language, such as BASIC or COBOL, into machine language.

Core. A carryover word (from the time when computers used ferrite cores, magnetically biased, to store information) for the computer's RAM memory. While most of today's computers use semiconductor (integrated-circuit chip) memories, previous generations of computers used arrays of ferrite cores which, depending on the direction they were magnetized, represented zeros and ones.

CP/M (Control Program for Microcomputers). A non-system specific operating system written by Digital Research. While originally written for the 8080 processor chip, it is now available in 8 bit, 16 bit (CPM/86) and multi-user versions (MP/M and MP/M II).

CPU (central processing unit). The part of the computer that controls and directs the flow of data throughout the entire computer system. In microcomputers, the entire CPU circuitry is contained on one integrated circuit (IC) chip.

CRT (Cathode Ray Terminal). Also called VDU (Video Display Unit) or "Screen." An I/O device consisting of a TV-like screen to present information to the user and a typewriter-like keyboard to accept information from the user.

Debug. To find and remove all malfunctions occurring in computer hardware or software.

Disk. A mass storage device on which information is magnetically stored. The medium supporting the magnetic coating can be a flexible plastic (used in floppy disks) or metal (used in rigid or hard disks).

Editor. A program used to create and modify text files (usually stored on disk). These text files are most commonly the source code for programs, but editors are sometimes used as part of a word processing system.

Execute. To perform an operation or program.

File. An organized assemblage of data. Files may consist of data records or programs. A helpful analogy is a filing cabinet. The cabinet itself is the storage device. The individual folders in the drawers are files, and the information contained in each folder is the records or data.

Firmware. Software that is implemented in read-only memory (ROM). This software is available as soon as the computer is turned on. Common firmware includes computer languages (such as BASIC), diagnostic routines which check out the machine on power-up, and bootstrap software to load the operating system.

Format. Refers to the arrangement of information (such as a record format), or the way data are stored on disk (disk format), or, under the CP/M operating system, the process of rendering a new disk usable by the system. This process is called formatting a blank disk.

Hardware. The physical parts of a data processing system. This can include a CRT, disk drives, printer, and so on.

High-Level Language. A programming language that creates machine language code from an English-like language. Examples of high-level languages are BASIC, FORTRAN, COBOL, and Pascal.

Input. Information which enters the data processing system. This can be by way of a typewriterlike keyboard or information stored on a device such as a disk.

Instruction. A direction for the computer to perform a function. Many instructions make up a program, which directs the computer to perform a number of tasks.

Interface. A subsystem of the computer which mediates between the CPU and a different part of the computer. Most common are I/O interfaces, which mediate between the CPU and I/O devices such as a printer or CRT. Other interfaces include disk interfaces and communication interfaces.

Interpreter. A type of high-level computer language where the program is translated into machine language, one line at a time, at run time (when the program is executed or run).

I/O. Input/output.

ISAM (index sequential access method). A method of accessing records on a disk file. One or more fields on the record are designated as "keys." The primary key should be a field that contains information unique to that record (such as a customer number, account number, etc.). A list of these keys and the location on the disk where the record containing this key is found is kept in a separate file called an "index file." When a program needs to access a particular disk record, it looks up the record's location in the index file (based on the record's key) and is able to go directly to the proper record on the disk. In addition, if a particular application requires that a file be accessed in a sorted order, many times it is possible to sort the index file rather than the file itself. As the index file is usually much smaller than the file it indexes, the sort can be accomplished much more rapidly.

Low-Level Language. A programming language whose structure and use closely correspond to the computer's actual machine code language.

LSI (large-scale integration). An electronic technology which permits integrated circuits to be constructed with many more components on them than was previously possible. This allows the construction of computers with many fewer chips than before, which in turn means that the computers can be made smaller, lighter, and less expensively than before. LSI technology is directly responsible for the current availability of personal computers.

Machine Language. The actual binary code (ones and zeros) that the computer uses internally to represent instructions and operations. All high- and low-level languages are translated into machine language before they are executed by the computer.

Mass Storage. The part of the computer used to store large amounts of data and programs not currently in use. Usually consists of magnetic storage on disks or tape.

Memory. The part of the computer used to store instructions (programs) and data. Memory may be random-access (RAM) or read-only (ROM) or mass storage (disk or tape).

Menu. A list of possible selections, presented to the operator on the screen of the CRT. The operator selects an operation or option by entering the selection number. A menu-driven application is considered "user-friendly" and cuts down on the chance of the operator inadvertently entering wrong information.

Microcomputer. A computer which has the CPU on one integrated circuit chip.

Microprocessor. An integrated circuit chip which contains all the electronic components of a computer's CPU.

Mnemonic. A word or letters representing a computer operation. For example, an assembler language mnemonic for the computer instruction "branch if equal" might be "BE."

Model. A symbolic representation of a process or object, generally in mathematical terms. By changing the values of the variables in a model, the effect on the model as a whole can be determined. Models are useful in forecasting and determining the effects of differing tax strategies (among other things).

Object Code. A program which has been translated into machine-executable format.

Operating System. Software (program) which mediates between the computer system and the operator, as well as the computer's peripherals.

Parallel I/O. A device where an entire character (byte) of information is sent or received at one time over eight (or more) data lines.

Peripheral Equipment. Additional equipment such as printers, CRTs, and mass storage units (disks and tapes) that are connected to the computer's main console.

Precision. The number of significant digits that the particular version of the computer language allows. For example, a language which allows 9-digit precision can handle numbers from $-9,999,999.99$ to $+9,999,999.99$, while a language with 12-digit precision can handle numbers from $-9,999,999,999.99$ to $+9,999,999,999.99$. Numbers outside the precision range of the language are handled in exponential form (e.g., $19,999,999.99$ would be converted to 1.9×10^7, assuming 9-digit precision).

Program. A set of machine instructions and routines to handle a data processing task.

RAM (random-access memory). The part of the computer's main memory that can be read from and/or written to. Every byte (character) in RAM can be individually accessed.

Random Access. A storage technique which allows a program to access, individually, any record in a disk file without having to read, sequentially, every record appearing before it.

Record. A component of a data file that contains a group of data that are interrelated. If a filing cabinet drawer is thought of as a *file*, then the individual folders can be thought of as *records*. [The data contained in the records (folders) could be thought of as *data fields*.]

ROM (read-only memory). A part of the computer's memory that contains information that can be read, but cannot be written to (i.e., the information is permanently in this memory). ROM is usually used to store information such as a built-in programming languge and bootstrap routines to load the computer's operating system upon power-up.

Routine. A set of program instructions to accomplish a particular task—for example, a routine to calculate gross wages would take hours worked and multiply them times the hourly rate.

Serial I/O. A device where a character (byte) is sent or received one *bit* (the units which make up the individual bytes or characters) at a time. Usually one byte (character) consists of eight *bits* of information. In addition, serial devices usually add several bits to the transmission to indicate the start and end of the particular character.

Sequential Access. A form of access that requires that records be read in sequential order [e.g., to access the 10th record in a file, you must have already accessed (read) records 1 through 9].

Software. The collection of instructions which "drive" the computer hardware. Application software consists of sets of instructions (programs) to accomplish tasks such as payroll or general ledger. System software consists of sets of instructions (programs) used to control the computer and its peripherals (such as the operating system).

Source Code. Instructions written in a source-level language (high- or low-level language such as BASIC or assembler language) which must be translated into object code (machine language) before the computer can execute them.

Storage Capacity. A measure of how much information can be maintained in a particular type or area of the computer's various memories.

Subroutine. A group of program instructions that can be used in more than one place in a program. For example, in a program that prints many numbers, the program might jump to a subroutine to format the number (put in the dollar sign and commas) instead of having to include the same program steps several times in the program. This technique not only structures the program better, but also allows the program to take up less space in the computer's memory.

Syntax. The formal structure of a computer language.

Terminal. An input/output device such as a CRT, teletypewriter, or printer.

Time-Sharing. A technique where several users can share the same computer equipment while it appears to each user that he or she is the only one using the system.

Utility Program. A program providing a feature not inherent in the computer's operating system or application software. For example, the CP/M operating system is usually supplied with several useful utilities such as STAT, which gives the user information on devices in the system (such as what files are on a disk and how large they are), and PIP (peripheral interchange program), which allows (among other features) files to be transferred from one device to another.

APPENDIXES

A. FEASIBILITY STUDY WORKSHEET

JOB AND JOB STEP	PERFORMED BY	COST/HOUR	ALTERNATIVES	COST

B. PRELIMINARY COST/BENEFIT ANALYSIS WORKSHEET

BENEFITS	COSTS

C. SYSTEM STUDY WORKSHEET

APPLICATION	RELATIVE IMPORTANCE	REQUIRED CAPACITIES	
		Now	Future

D. SAMPLE SOFTWARE CONTRACT

Appendix D contains a sample software contract and excerpts from the specification documents which are mentioned in (and were part of) the agreement. For the sake of brevity (the actual documental is 47 pages long!) I have included several parts of the document. The actual specification document which accompanied (and become part of) the agreement contained system flow charts, PERT charts, layouts for reports and data entry screens as well as documentation standards to be followed in both the programming and the system documentation. The following materials are reproduced through the courtesy of IDEA TECHNOLOGY.

Author's Note: The enclosed document is presented for illustration only. Both the author, publisher, and IDEA TECHNOLOGY, disclaim any and all responsibility as to its suitability or legality. Please consult with your attorney before making up, or signing, any agreements.

D(a) SECTION I: INTRODUCTION

DOCUMENT PURPOSE

This document is intended to specify requirements and intended approaches to be followed in establishing a multi-user microcomputer based facility for ____ ____ ____, ____. This facility will be used (at least initially) by _____ for the following purposes (with other applications to be added at later dates):

A. *Front-end to TFS:* This function will allow multiple users to have full-screen, interactive data-entry and verification (edit) for DEC 10 based financial and MIS Systems. The specific data-entry functions are detailed in the section of this document titled "SOFTWARE."

B. *Accounts Payable:* As current TFS contains only a limited

Accounts Payable, a full-featured "Packaged" Accounts Payable will be installed. Files generated and maintained by this package will be reformatted into a format acceptable to TFS.

C. *Software Development:* This facility will also be used by _____ to develop software to be utilized by _____ Clients on their own in-house microcomputers.

D. *Stand-alone Applications:* Each workstation in the network is a full-function computer. This allows each workstation to run not only applications which have been off-loaded from the network, but also to run applications which may be hardware specific.

MICRO-BASED FRONT END SYSTEM

Applications to Be Implemented:

1. Accounting Journal Entry:
   (a) Fixed format journal entry (standard adjustments)
   (b) Free-form journal entry
   (c) Data entry edit report
   (d) General Journal (report)
   (e) Create journal transaction file and transmit to DEC 10

2. Cash Receipts:
   (a) Search/match checks to invoices
   (b) Data entry—cash receipts
   (c) Cash receipts edit report
   (d) Cash receipts journal
   (e) Cash receipts exception report (details partially or incorrectly paid invoices)
   (f) Create journal transaction file and transmit to DEC 10

3. Special Invoicing: (Invoicing now being done manually)
   (a) Data entry—special invoice
   (b) Edit report
   (c) Generate (print) special invoices and journal
   (d) Create journal transaction file and transmit to DEC 10

4. Budget Adjustment:
   (a) Budget adjustments—Data entry
   (b) Edit report
   (c) Create transaction file and transmit to DEC 10

5. Accounts Payable Enhancements to TFS:
   - (a) Data entry—check requests and authorization to pay
   - (b) Edit report
   - (c) Create transaction file and transmit to DEC 10
   - (d) Data entry—purchases
   - (e) Edit report—purchases
   - (f) Generate purchase journal
   - (g) Create transaction file and transmit to DEC 10

6. Ad Hoc Reporting:
   - (a) Use of Access/80 to produce ad hoc management reports

7. Software Development Capability:
   - (a) Application development software used to develop prior applications (1 through 6) will remain on the system. This will give immediate micro-based software development capability.

D(b) SECTION VI: SUGGESTED MAJOR MILESTONES AND PAYMENT SCHEDULE

MILESTONE	AMOUNT DUE	APPROXIMATE TIME FRAME
(1) Acceptance of System Specifications	$ 1000.00	2–3 weeks
(2) Demonstrate two-way file transfer capability and file format conversion capability	$ 1000.00	5–6 weeks
(3) Demonstrate Vendor Search	$ 625.00	6–7 weeks
(4) Demonstrate Data Entry and Edit Reports	$ 1500.00	8–11 weeks
(5) Demonstrate Single-user hard-disk system	$ 1500.00	11–14 weeks
(6) Demonstrate multi-user system	$ 1000.00	12–15 weeks
(7) Deliver equipment to _____ set-up and Demonstration	$ 625.00	12–16 weeks
(8) Finish training	$ 1500.00	13–17 weeks
(9) Acceptance of System by _____	$ 1750.00	15–20 weeks
	$10500.00	

NOTES:

1. Demonstrations above numbered (2) through (6) will be held at the office of IDEA TECHNOLOGY
2. System Specifications will be deemed to be accepted when signed by both _____ and IDEA TECHNOLOGY
3. The retainer of $500.00 will be applied to first amount due

---

March 30, 19XX

_____
Chairman
_____
_____
_____

Dear _____

This letter will confirm the engagement of IDEA TECHNOLOGY (Divsion of Microtechnology Associates, Incorporated) to assist the _____ in developing a microcomputer-based network as detailed in the preceding pages of this document.

Our fee for these services will be Ten Thousand, Five Hundred Dollars ($10,500.00) to be paid as detailed in Section VI— Schedule of Milestones.

The terms of our engagement shall be as follows:

(1)   "Document," as referred to in this agreement, refers to the attached _____ _____ Multi-user Microcomputer Data-Entry and Development System; System Specifications and Agreement, including Appendixes A, B, C.

(2)   Hardware shall be implemented through "Phase Two" as detailed in the "Hardware" section of this document (multi-user environment with workstation equipment from a single vendor). Implementation of "Phase Three" (multi-user Multi-vendor environment) is not included in this agreement and must be separately negotiated at a later date.

(3)   Software applications shall be implemented as described in this document.

(4)   _____ recognizes, and agrees, that all times quoted in this document are estimates, and that IDEA TECHNOLOGY has prepared these estimates based on various manufacturers' published specifications as to per-performance and availability. _____ further agrees not to hold IDEA TECHNOLOGY liable for delays in meeting agreed upon milestones caused by failure of required hardware or software not developed by IDEA TECHNOLOGY to meet published specifications as to performance or availability.

(5)   In consideration of Section 4, IDEA TECHNOLOGY agrees, that should it become necessary due to circumstances detailed in Section 4, it will provide, at no additional charge, up to an additional 30 man/days of service above the 42 man/days detailed in Appendix A. Should additional time, in addition to the above mentioned time, become necessary, _____ agrees to pay IDEA TECHNOLOGY for this time at a rate of One Hundred and Twenty Five Dollars ($125.00) per man/day. Should this become necessary, the additional time will be billed and documented by IDEA TECHNOLOGY and such amounts may be paid by _____ into an escrow account established with an uninvolved third party to be agreed upon by both _____ and IDEA TECHNOLOGY. Additionally, this escrow will be held until a satisfactory conclusion of this agreement is achieved.

(6)   IDEA TECHNOLOGY agrees that all software developed by IDEA TECHNOLOGY under the terms of this agreement is the property of _____ and IDEA TECHNOLOGY furthermore agrees to sign a non-disclosure agreement if required by _____ and to waive all future rights to such software if developed for _____.

(7)   _____ agrees that all commercially available software packages required by IDEA TECHNOLOGY to complete this agreement shall be purchased by _____. _____ shall retain all rights to this software as detailed in the licensing agreements with the producer/ supplier of said software.

(8)   _____ agrees that IDEA TECHNOLOGY may, with written permission from _____, act as _____ agent in the purchase of required software. If IDEA

TECHNOLOGY acts for _____ in this fashion, then IDEA TECHNOLOGY shall purchase said software and will bill, and be reimbursed by, _____ for said software. Such reimbursement is due and payable upon receipt by _____ of request for payment. Any software purchased by IDEA TECHNOLOGY under this arrangement shall be deemed to be the property of _____ and all original documentation and media will be conveyed to _____ at or before the conclusion of this agreement.

(9)   _____ agrees that the consideration detailed in this agreement is for the services of IDEA TECHNOLOGY and its employees. Incidental expenses incurred by IDEA TECHNOLOGY and its employees are not included and will be separately billed to, and paid by, _____ on a monthly basis. These expenses include, but are not limited to, telephone charges incurred in the performance of this agreement, and documentation required by IDEA TECHNOLOGY to evaluate the appropriateness of commercially available hardware or software for use in fulfilling this agreement.

IDEA TECHNOLOGY agrees to obtain, from _____, written permission before incurring on _____ behalf any one expense in excess of fifty dollars.

IDEA TECHNOLOGY further agrees that all documentation obtained for evaluation purposes, paid for by _____, is _____ property, and possession will revert to _____ on or before completion of this agreement.

(10)   _____ agrees that _____ shall be responsible for obtaining any hardware required. IDEA TECHNOLOGY will assist, if required in this purchase, but will not provide any hardware.

(11)   _____ agrees to lend IDEA TECHNOLOGY any and all hardware obtained for this project as detailed in this document. _____ shall retain all rights to any equipment it loans IDEA TECHNOLOGY. IDEA TECHNOLOGY agrees to return to _____, at its offices at _____ Avenue, New York, N.Y., any and all equipment it has borrowed from _____. IDEA TECHNOLOGY agrees it will make such return within

twenty four hours of receipt of such a request in writing from _____.

(12) _____ agrees to pay IDEA TECHNOLOGY for its services as per the Schedule of Milestones (Section VI) included in this document. A milestone shall be considered achieved when a particular capability, as detailed in the schedule in this document, has been demonstrated to _____ or an agent of _____. All demonstrations, unless otherwise specified, are to be held at the offices of IDEA TECHNOLOGY. _____ agrees to attend such demonstrations within seven days of written notification by IDEA TECHNOLOGY that a designated milestone has been achieved. Such demonstrations shall take place at a mutually agreed upon day and time within the required seven day period.

_____ further agrees that payment, as detailed in attached milestone schedule, is due and payable when a milestone has been achieved and demonstrated.

IDEA TECHNOLOGY agrees to extend to _____ a grace period of at least ten days to make such payment, although additional grace time may be granted to _____ at IDEA TECHNOLOGY's option.

(13) In the event _____ has not made a payment required under the terms of this agreement within thirty days after such payment becomes due, IDEA TECHNOLOGY reserves the right to suspend all work required under this agreement until such time as payment has been received by IDEA TECHNOLOGY.

(14) In the event that _____ has not made a payment required under the terms of this agreement within sixty days after such payment becomes due, this agreement shall be considered breached.

(15) _____ agrees that IDEA TECHNOLOGY shall have no responsibility or liability for any hardware purchased for this project or hardware _____ has possession of prior to this agreement.

_____ shall purchase required hardware from a vendor of _____ choice and will resolve any hardware related problems with this vendor.

_____ shall furthermore be responsible for any repair and or maintenance on such hardware.

AGREED TO ON THIS _____ DAY OF _____, 1982

SIGNED: _____   SIGNED: _____
TITLE: _____   TITLE: _____

_____, _____   IDEA TECHNOLOGY
_____ Avenue   Spring Valley, N.Y. 10977
New York, N.Y. 10016

E. SAMPLE COMPUTERIZED GENERAL LEDGER SYSTEM REPORTS

The following sample reports will provide you with a good idea of the format and versatility of computerized general ledger systems. The reports presented here were generated with the "General Ledger Accounting System" from BPI Systems, Inc. While the package is not an accountant-oriented "write-up" system, because of its ease of use, availability on many different systems, and versatility, it is being widely used by accountants. All of the reports are reprinted through the courtesy of BPI Systems, Inc., Austin, Texas.

Sample reports included here are:
Balance Sheet
Income Statement
Trial Balance
General Ledger
Accounts Receivable Ledger
Accounts Payable Ledger
Monthly, Quarterly, and Year-to-date Payroll Register
General Journal
Cash Disbursements Journal
Cash Receipts Journal
Cash Sales Journal
Merchandise Purchased Journal
Invoice Register

```
                    A CORNER GROCERY STORE
                       BALANCE SHEET
                        MAY 31, 1979


ASSETS
    CURRENT ASSETS
        CASH ON HAND                    533.29
        CASH ON DEPOSIT              15,034.05
        ACCOUNTS RECEIVABLE           2,465.70
        COUPONS RECEIVABLE               53.18
        EMPLOYEE ADVANCES               574.50
        INVENTORY                    17,347.61
            TOTAL CURRENT ASSETS                        36,008.33

    FIXED ASSETS
        MACHINERY AND EQUIPMENT      58,104.12
        ACCUMULATED DEPRECIATION     <3,836.48>
            TOTAL FIXED ASSETS                          54,267.64

    OTHER ASSETS
        DEPOSITS                      7,466.58
        FRANCHISE FEES                5,500.00
        PREPAID RENT                  1,500.00
        PREPAID INTEREST             11,826.70
            TOTAL OTHER ASSETS                          26,293.28
                                                       ---------------
            TOTAL ASSETS                               116,569.25
                                                       ===============


LIABILITIES
    CURRENT LIABILITIES
        ACCOUNTS PAYABLE              8,688.75
        SALES TAX PAYABLE             1,576.01
        FICA PAYABLE                    131.22
        WITHHOLDING TAX PAYABLE         194.83
            TOTAL CURRENT LIABILITIES                   10,590.81

    LONG TERM LIABILITIES
        NOTES PAYABLE-FOOD           14,426.99
        NOTES PAYABLE-EQUIP.         52,547.82
            TOTAL LONG TERM LIABILITIES                 66,974.81
                                                       ---------------
            TOTAL LIABILITIES                           77,565.62

CAPITAL
        CAPITAL STOCK                24,500.00
        RETAINED EARNINGS            14,503.63

            TOTAL CAPITAL                               39,003.63
                                                       ---------------
            TOTAL LIABILITIES & CAPITAL                116,569.25
                                                       ===============
```

```
              A CORNER GROCERY STORE                    60
           PROFIT AND LOSS STATEMENT
              MAY 31, 1979

                    CURRENT    %      YEAR-TO-DATE    %


INCOME
   SALES-GROCERY          38,445.41              170,040.02
                        ------------             ------------
      TOTAL              38,445.41  100.0        170,040.02  100.0

COST OF SALES
   COST OF SALES         26,332.26   68.5        118,711.68   69.8
                        ------------             ------------
GROSS PROFIT            12,113.15   31.5         51,328.34   30.2

EXPENSES
   SALARIES AND WAGES     2,844.40    7.4         14,992.95    8.8
   FRANCHISE FEES         1,624.86    4.2          7,047.74    4.1
   LAUNDRY AND UNIFORMS       0.00    0.0             25.40    0.0
   CASH OVER/SHORT        <136.81>  <0.4>           <47.21>  <0.0>
   RENT                   1,500.00    3.9          7,500.00    4.4
   UTILITIES                734.46    1.9          5,358.09    3.2
   TELEPHONE                 46.18    0.1            214.97    0.1
   GARBAGE SERVICE            0.00    0.0            127.00    0.1
   REPAIRS AND MAINTENANCE   81.73    0.2            374.06    0.2
   PAYROLL TAXES            215.11    0.6          1,429.90    0.8
   SUPPLIES                  98.50    0.3            769.83    0.5
   INTEREST EXPENSE         327.37    0.9          1,804.66    1.1
   INSURANCE                386.00    1.0          1,158.86    0.7
   LEGAL AND PROFESSIONAL     0.00    0.0             80.00    0.0
   POSTAGE AND OFFICE SUPPLIES 1.58   0.0              3.16    0.0
   MACHINERY AND EQUIP. RENTAL 0.00   0.0             15.84    0.0
   HOSPITALIZATION INSURANCE   0.00   0.0            428.52    0.3
   LOSSES ON BAD CHECKS       6.50    0.0            136.04    0.1
   SECURITY SERVICE          27.00    0.1            135.00    0.1
   DEPRECIATION             479.56    1.2          2,397.80    1.4
   MISCELLANEOUS EXPENSE      9.50    0.0             21.50    0.0
                        ------------             ------------
      TOTAL               8,245.94   21.4         43,974.11   25.9
                        ------------             ------------
INCOME <LOSS>            3,867.21   10.1          7,354.23    4.3

OTHER INCOME
   GASOLINE COMMISSIONS     680.81    1.8          2,486.36    1.5
   OTHER INCOME              43.25    0.1            217.35    0.1
                        ------------             ------------
      TOTAL                 724.06    1.9          2,703.71    1.6
                        ------------             ------------
NET INCOME <LOSS>        4,591.27   11.9         10,057.94    5.9
                        ============             ============
```

Reports Courtesy of BPI Systems, Inc.—Austin, Texas

ACCT NO	ACCOUNT NAME	FOLIO	BALANCE FORWARD	CURRENT MONTH	BALANCE
1010	CASH ON HAND		416.54		
	JE # 31	GJ		668.89CR	
	MONTHLY C-S SUMMARY	CS		13,440.56CR	
	MONTHLY C-S SUMMARY	CS		14,226.20	
					533.29
1020	CASH ON DEPOSIT		8,535.30		
	JE # 32	GJ		11.89CR	
	JE # 34	GJ		65.00CR	
	JE # 35	GJ		58.50	
	MONTHLY C-S SUMMARY	CS		37,675.28	
	MONTHLY C-S SUMMARY	CS		88.00	
	CHECKS FOR MONTH	CD		33,767.55CR	
	SALES SUMMARY	IR		0.00	
	CASH RECEIPTS SUMMARY	CR		2,521.41	
					15,034.05
1110	ACCOUNTS RECEIVABLE		2,709.92		
	SALES SUMMARY	IR		2,277.19	
	CASH RECEIPTS SUMMARY	CR		2,521.41CR	
					2,465.70
1120	COUPONS RECEIVABLE		56.32		
	JE # 31	GJ		14.60CR	
	MONTHLY C-S SUMMARY	CS		11.46	
					53.18
1130	EMPLOYEE ADVANCES		574.50		574.50
1150	INVENTORY		20,235.00		
	JE # 36	GJ		2,887.39CR	
					17,347.61
1220	MACHINERY AND EQUIPMENT		58,104.12		58,104.12
1250	ACCUMULATED DEPRECIATIO		3,356.92CR		
	JE # 33	GJ		479.56CR	
					3,836.48CR
1400	DEPOSITS		7,466.58		7,466.58
1410	FRANCHISE FEES		5,500.00		5,500.00
1420	PREPAID RENT		1,500.00		1,500.00
1430	PREPAID INTEREST		12,068.00		
	FIRST NATIONAL BANK	CK # 522		241.30CR	
					11,826.70

AS OF
05/31/79   ACCOUNTS RECEIVABLE LEDGER

CUSTOMER NO -- NAME	FOLIO	BALANCE FORWARD	CURRENT MONTH	BALANCE
1 GUZMAN, ARNOLD		98. 62		
INVOICE # 603	IR		58. 03	
05/12/79	CR		98. 62CR	
				58. 03
2 FOSBECK, DONALD G.		67. 22		
05/25/79	CR		67. 22CR	
				0. 00
3 FOSTER, JOE T.		119. 68		
INVOICE # 599	IR		42. 85	
05/14/79	CR		119. 68CR	
				42. 85
4 HUNTER, THOMAS		22. 80		
INVOICE # 594	IR		38. 65	
INVOICE # 598	IR		73. 73	
INVOICE # 608	IR		89. 10	
05/03/79	CR		22. 80CR	
				201. 48
5 MOODY, CYNTHIA		110. 16		
INVOICE # 591	IR		37. 90	
INVOICE # 623	IR		69. 11	
05/09/79	CR		110. 16CR	
				107. 01
6 MONTGOMERY, DARRELL		167. 50		
05/14/79	CR		167. 50CR	
				0. 00
7 OGELSBY, W. H.		88. 60		
INVOICE # 597	IR		10. 52	
05/22/79	CR		88. 60CR	
				10. 52
8 COLLIER, A. W.		101. 89		
INVOICE # 617	IR		74. 54	
05/25/79	CR		101. 89CR	
				74. 54
9 BROWN, CHARLES		19. 80		
INVOICE # 616	IR		34. 20	
05/01/79	CR		19. 80CR	
				34. 20
10 HACKETT, ARNOLD		106. 82		
INVOICE # 589	IR		24. 51	
INVOICE # 602	IR		47. 59	
INVOICE # 628	IR		84. 80	

```
AS OF
05/31/79                     ACCOUNTS PAYABLE LEDGER
```

VENDOR NO -- NAME	FOLIO	BALANCE FORWARD	CURRENT MONTH	BALANCE
1 AMALGAMATED PRODUCE CO.		416. 20CR		
CHECK # 397	CD		416. 20	
INVOICE # 6723	MP		129. 30CR	
INVOICE # 6799	MP		246. 65CR	
INVOICE # 6833	MP		141. 68CR	
				517. 63CR
2 SAMSON SAUSAGE CO.		189. 62CR		
CHECK # 424	CD		189. 62	
INVOICE # 1367	MP		62. 50CR	
INVOICE # 1480	MP		115. 88CR	
				178. 38CR
3 AMERICAN BISCUIT CO.		178. 15CR		
CHECK # 403	CD		178. 15	
CHECK # 490	CD		96. 50	
INVOICE # 2987	MP		96. 50CR	
INVOICE # 3088	MP		110. 65CR	
				110. 65CR
4 SWANSON POTATO CHIPS		492. 18CR		
CHECK # 463	CD		492. 18	
INVOICE # 10267	MP		213. 20CR	
INVOICE # 10303	MP		415. 60CR	
				628. 80CR
5 SUPER COLA BOTTLING CO.		689. 68CR		
CHECK # 419	CD		689. 68	
INVOICE # 10729	MP		233. 50CR	
INVOICE # 11102	MP		223. 86CR	
INVOICE # 11623	MP		291. 48CR	
				748. 84CR
6 NEUMAN WINE CO.		292. 80CR		
CHECK # 415	CD		292. 80	
INVOICE # 10478	MP		167. 50CR	
INVOICE # 10560	MP		99. 68CR	
				267. 18CR
7 MILTON BOTTLING CO.		170. 24CR		
CHECK # 402	CD		170. 24	
INVOICE # 13966	MP		106. 29CR	
INVOICE # 14102	MP		198. 67CR	
				304. 96CR
8 MRS. SMITH'S BAKERIES		124. 19CR		
CHECK # 422	CD		124. 19	
CHECK # 459	CD		89. 97	
CHECK # 480	CD		72. 68	
INVOICE # 36290	MP		89. 97CR	

Reports Courtesy of BPI Systems, Inc.—Austin, Texas

A CORNER GROCERY STORE

AS OF
05/31/79

MONTHLY PAYROLL REGISTER

REFERENCE	GROSS PAY	F. I. C. A.	F. I. T.	OTHER DED.	NET PAY

EMPLOYEE # 101: MARY LANCASTER

CD 05/04/79 407	87.00	5.26-	4.00-		77.74
CD 05/11/79 439	87.00	5.33-	4.00-		77.67
CD 05/19/79 482	87.00	5.33-	4.00-		77.67
CD 05/27/79 509	87.00	5.33-	4.00-		77.67
MONTH	348.00	21.25-	16.00-	0.00	310.75
QUARTER	1,044.00	67.55-	58.50-	0.00	917.95
YEAR-TO-DATE	2,138.60	115.85-	124.69-	0.00	1,898.06

EMPLOYEE # 102: JAMES MONTGOMERY

CD 05/04/79 408	200.00	12.10-	14.30-		173.60
CD 05/11/79 440	200.00	12.26-	14.30-		173.44
CD 05/19/79 483	200.00	12.26-	14.30-		173.44
CD 05/27/79 510	200.00	12.26-	14.30-		173.44
MONTH	800.00	48.88-	57.20-	0.00	693.92
QUARTER	2,400.00	148.98-	154.96-	0.00	2,096.06
YEAR-TO-DATE	5,000.00	366.08-	312.26-	0.00	4,321.66

EMPLOYEE # 103: JACK RYDEN

CD 05/06/79 411	200.00	12.10-	24.70-		163.20
CD 05/13/79 443	200.00	12.26-	24.70-		163.04
CD 05/19/79 486	200.00	12.26-	24.70-		163.04
CD 05/27/79 513	200.00	12.26-	24.70-		163.04
MONTH	800.00	48.88-	98.80-	0.00	652.32
QUARTER	2,400.00	246.48-	196.56-	0.00	1,956.96
YEAR-TO-DATE	5,000.00	567.58-	353.86-	0.00	4,078.56

EMPLOYEE # 106: WILLIAM P. HAGEN

CD 05/19/79 485	40.60	2.49-	1.20-		36.91
MONTH	40.60	2.49-	1.20-	0.00	36.91
QUARTER	81.20	3.69-	3.69-	0.00	73.82
YEAR-TO-DATE	1,395.15	152.79-	77.55-	0.00	1,164.81

EMPLOYEE # 107: THOMAS REID

CD 05/06/79 412	20.30		1.23-		19.07
CD 05/13/79 444	13.05	0.80-	0.00		12.25
CD 05/19/79 487	37.70	2.31-	0.00		35.39
MONTH	71.05	3.11-	1.23-	0.00	66.71
QUARTER	213.15	4.34-	8.68-	0.00	200.13
YEAR-TO-DATE	817.70	4.34-	45.26-	0.00	768.10

```
AS OF
05/31/79              QUARTER AND YEAR-TO-DATE

REFERENCE          GROSS PAY     F. I. C. A.     F. I. T.    OTHER DED.    NET PAY
--------------------------------------------------------------------------------

EMPLOYEE # 101:   MARY LANCASTER

        QUARTER    1,044.00        .67.55-        58.50-       0.00       917.95
     YEAR-TO-DATE  2,138.60       115.85-        124.69-       0.00     1,898.06

EMPLOYEE # 102:   JAMES MONTGOMERY

        QUARTER    2,400.00       148.98-        154.96-       0.00     2,096.06
     YEAR-TO-DATE  5,000.00       366.08-        312.26-       0.00     4,321.66

EMPLOYEE # 103:   JACK RYDEN

        QUARTER    2,400.00       246.48-        196.56-       0.00     1,956.96
     YEAR-TO-DATE  5,000.00       567.58-        353.86-       0.00     4,078.56

EMPLOYEE # 104:   DAVID LUNSFORD

        QUARTER       0.00          0.00           0.00        0.00         0.00
     YEAR-TO-DATE    69.75          0.00           4.22-       0.00        65.53

EMPLOYEE # 105:   JANE P. SMITH

        QUARTER       0.00          0.00           0.00        0.00         0.00
     YEAR-TO-DATE   121.35          6.30-          7.34-       0.00       107.71

EMPLOYEE # 106:   WILLIAM P. HAGEN

        QUARTER      81.20          3.69-          3.69-       0.00        73.82
     YEAR-TO-DATE  1,395.15       152.79-         77.55-       0.00     1,164.81

EMPLOYEE # 107:   THOMAS REID

        QUARTER     213.15          4.34-          8.68-       0.00       200.13
     YEAR-TO-DATE   817.70          4.34-         45.26-       0.00       768.10

EMPLOYEE # 108:   JAMES F. STANLEY

        QUARTER     588.70         39.55-         38.39-       0.00       510.76
     YEAR-TO-DATE  1,091.85        62.55-         68.84-       0.00       960.46

EMPLOYEE # 109:   KENNETH HOBBY

        QUARTER    1,680.00       164.61-        133.62-       0.00     1,381.77
     YEAR-TO-DATE  2,076.80       209.01-        157.63-       0.00     1,710.16

EMPLOYEE # 110:   ARTHUR PRESTON

        QUARTER     126.15          2.58-          5.16-       0.00       118.41
     YEAR-TO-DATE   126.15          2.58-          5.16-       0.00       118.41
```

A CORNER GROCERY STORE

GENERAL JOURNAL
AS OF 05/31/79

DATE	JE#	ACCOUNT	DEBIT	CREDIT
05/31/79	31	7021 OTHER INCOME	1,834.33	
		1120 COUPONS RECEIVABLE		14.60
		7011 GASOLINE COMMISSIONS		1,021.21
		4901 COST OF SALES		129.63
		1010 CASH ON HAND		668.89
		TO DITRIBUTE 'OTHER INCOME' FROM CASH SALES SUMMARY		
05/31/79	32	4011 SALES-GROCERY	11.89	
		1020 CASH ON DEPOSIT		11.89
		TO ENTER DEPOSIT CORRECTIONS FOR MONTH PER BANK STATEMENT		
05/31/79	33	5781 DEPRECIATION	479.56	
		1250 ACCUMULATED DEPRECIATION		479.56
		DEPRECIATION PROVISION FOR MAY '79		
05/31/79	34	5751 LOSSES ON BAD CHECKS	65.00	
		1020 CASH ON DEPOSIT		65.00
		TO ENTER BAD CHECK LOSSES FOR MONTH		
05/31/79	35	1020 CASH ON DEPOSIT	58.50	
		5751 LOSSES ON BAD CHECKS		58.50
		TO ENTER BAD CHECK COLLECTIONS FPOR MONTH		
05/31/79	36	4901 COST OF SALES	2,887.39	
		1150 INVENTORY		2,887.39
		TO ADJUST INVENTORY TO PHYSICAL INVENTORY TAKEN 5/31/79		

A CORNER GROCERY STORE

CASH DISBURSEMENTS
AS OF 05/31/79

DATE	PAYEE	CHECK NUMBER	ACCT NO.	SUB ACCT NO.	DETAIL	NET AMT.
5/01/79	JONES REALTY CO.	389	5561			1,500.00
05/01/79	STATE TREASURER	390	2030			488.74
05/02/79	CENTRAL FOOD MARTS	391	5531			305.08
05/02/79	WATSON DISTRIBUTING CO.	392	4901			51.30
05/02/79	WHOLESALE BEER DIST. CO.	393	4901			21.20
05/02/79	JACKSON FOOD SERVICE	394	4901			27.50
05/02/79	SMITH DISTRIBUTING CO.	395	4901			199.50
05/03/79	SMITH DISTRIBUTING CO.	396	4901			199.50
05/03/79	AMALGAMATED PRODUCE CO.	397	2010	1		416.20
05/03/79	WATSON DISTRIBUTING CO.	398	4901			225.00
05/03/79	JONES FARMS	399	2010	11		67.20
05/03/79	JONES DISTRIBUTING CO.	400	4901			469.00
05/03/79	STATE WIDE DIST. CO.	401	4901			487.31
05/03/79	MILTON BOTTLING CO.	402	2010	7		170.24
05/03/79	AMERICAN BISCUIT CO.	403	2010	3		178.15
05/03/79	RICCO'S PIZZA	404	2010	12		95.50
05/03/79	WATSON DISTRIBUTING CO.	405	4901			317.99
05/04/79	WHOLESALE BEER DIST. CO.	406	4901			203.80
05/04/79	MARY LANCASTER	407	5521	101	87.00	
			2050	101	4.00-	
			2040	101	5.26-	77.74
05/04/79	JAMES MONTGOMERY	408	5521	102	200.00	
			2050	102	14.30-	
			2040	102	12.10-	173.60
05/04/79	KENNETH HOBBY	409	5521	109	140.00	
			2050	109	16.30-	
			2040	109	8.47-	115.23
05/04/79	VOID	410				

INVOICE REGISTER
AS OF 05/31/79

DATE	CUST NO.	CUSTOMER NAME	INVOICE NUMBER	ACCT. NUMBER	DETAIL	NET AMT
05/01/79	10	HACKETT, ARNOLD	589	4011	23. 80	
				2030	0. 71	24. 51
05/01/79	20	HOWARD, WILLIAM H.	590	4011	16. 89	
				2030	0. 51	17. 40
05/02/79	5	MOODY, CYNTHIA	591	4011	36. 80	
				2030	1. 10	37. 90
05/03/79	23	SILLS, FRANK	592	4011	42. 10	
				2030	1. 26	43. 36
05/03/79	28	MONROE, KEN	593	4011	22. 95	
				2030	0. 69	23. 64
05/04/79	4	HUNTER, THOMAS	594	4011	37. 52	
				2030	1. 13	38. 65
05/05/79	14	YOUNGBLOOD, JACK A.	595	4011	61. 50	
				2030	1. 85	63. 35
05/05/79	11	NUNN, ALTON B.	596	4011	52. 21	
				2030	1. 57	53. 78
05/05/79	7	OGELSBY, W. H.	597	4011	10. 20	
				2030	0. 32	10. 52
05/07/79	4	HUNTER, THOMAS	598	4011	71. 58	
				2030	2. 15	73. 73
05/08/79	3	FOSTER, JOE T.	599	4011	41. 60	
				2030	1. 25	42. 85
05/08/79	25	PARKER, JAMES	600	4011	29. 10	
				2030	0. 87	29. 97
05/09/79	27	MOLLOY, JOHN	601	4011	33. 50	
				2030	1. 00	34. 50
05/10/79	10	HACKETT, ARNOLD	602	4011	46. 20	
				2030	1. 39	47. 59
05/10/79	1	GUZMAN, ARNOLD	603	4011	56. 34	
				2030	1. 69	58. 03
05/11/79	21	CURTIS, JOHN	604	4011	31. 10	
				2030	0. 93	32. 03
05/11/79	19	NOLEN, A. B.	605	4011	18. 79	
				2030	0. 56	19. 35

CASH RECEIPTS JOURNAL
AS OF 05/31/79

DATE	CUST. NUMBER	CUSTOMER NAME	DETAIL	NET AMOUNT
05/01/79	16	RAY, WILLIAM H.	52.18	
	9	BROWN, CHARLES	19.80	71.98
05/03/79	4	HUNTER, THOMAS	22.80	
	19	NOLEN, A. B.	89.20	112.00
05/06/79	13	HORNSBY, MICHAEL	189.65	
	22	WATKINS, DOROTHY	100.00	
	15	YOUNG, WILLIAM	46.27	335.92
05/09/79	5	MOODY, CYNTHIA	110.16	
	25	PARKER, JAMES	96.31	
	27	MOLLOY, JOHN	110.21	
	28	MONROE, KEN	60.00	376.68
05/12/79	1	GUZMAN, ARNOLD	98.62	
	20	HOWARD, WILLIAM H.	101.60	200.22
05/14/79	6	MONTGOMERY, DARRELL	167.50	
	3	FOSTER, JOE T.	119.68	287.18
05/18/79	23	SILLS, FRANK	10.66	
	24	READ, TONY	81.60	
	26	MYERS, JERRY	44.80	137.06
05/22/79	7	OGELSBY, W. H.		88.60
05/25/79	8	COLLIER, A. W.	101.89	
	2	FOSBECK, DONALD G.	67.22	
	10	HACKETT, ARNOLD	106.82	275.93
05/29/79	11	NUNN, ALTON B.	121.20	
	12	CASTLEBERRY, RAYMOND	206.20	
	17	PERRY, ALEXANDER	175.10	
	21	CURTIS, JOHN	133.34	635.84
		TOTAL		2,521.41

MERCHANDISE PURCHASED JOURNAL
AS OF 05/31/79

DATE	VENDOR NO.	VENDOR NAME	INVOICE NUMBER	ACCT NUMBER	DETAIL	NET AMT
05/01/79	1	AMALGAMATED PRODUCE C	6723	4901		129.30
05/01/79	6	NEUMAN WINE CO.	10478	4901		167.50
05/02/79	15	WHOLESALE GROCERY CO.	33629	4901		1,029.67
05/03/79	10	NATU-WHEAT BREAD CO.	5628	4901		67.50
05/03/79	2	SAMSON SAUSAGE CO.	1367	4901		62.50
05/04/79	4	SWANSON POTATO CHIPS	10267	4901		213.20
05/05/79	3	AMERICAN BISCUIT CO.	2987	4901		96.50
05/05/79	7	MILTON BOTTLING CO.	13966	4901		106.29
05/06/79	5	SUPER COLA BOTTLING C	10729	4901		233.50
05/07/79	16	JIM'S SNACKS	1062	4901		37.95
05/08/79	8	MRS. SMITH'S BAKERIES	36290	4901		89.97
05/08/79	9	NATIONAL WINE CO.	4468	4901		102.96
05/09/79	11	JONES FARMS	1367	4901		44.96
05/10/79	12	RICCO'S PIZZA	2951	4901		46.50
05/11/79	13	CROWN BOTTLING CO.	33362	4901		298.99
05/12/79	14	TOP-FLITE MILK CO.	11692	4901		398.66
05/13/79	1	AMALGAMATED PRODUCE C	6799	4901		246.65
05/14/79	6	NEUMAN WINE CO.	10560	4901		99.68
05/15/79	10	NATU-WHEAT BREAD CO.	5785	4901		45.88
05/15/79	8	MRS. SMITH'S BAKERIES	36485	4901		72.68
05/16/79	7	MILTON BOTTLING CO.	14102	4901		198.67
05/16/79	11	JONES FARMS	1480	4901		88.68
05/17/79	12	RICCO'S PIZZA	3021	4901		29.50
05/17/79	14	TOP-FLITE MILK CO.	1726	4901		482.97
05/18/79	15	WHOLESALE GROCERY CO.	34001	4901	1,798.37	
				5631	98.50	1,896.87

A CORNER GROCERY STORE   93

CASH SALES JOURNAL

	05/01/79	05/02/79	05/03/79	05/04/79
INCOMING CASH				
SALES TAX	31. 67-	11. 53-	22. 68-	26. 02-
BOTTLE DEP. REC.	16. 65-	10. 25-	15. 80-	20. 60-
SALES-GROCERY	1, 126. 57-	917. 47-	960. 28-	1, 111. 53-
OTHER INCOME	0. 00	0. 00	14. 60-	0. 00
OPENING CASH	426. 51-	354. 57-	345. 64-	417. 99-
CASH PD. OUT & DEPOS				
CASH PURCHASES	28. 10	97. 85	16. 40	30. 53
COUPONS REC.	0. 25	0. 00	0. 83	1. 15
MISCELL. EXP.	0. 00	0. 00	0. 00	0. 00
CASH DEPOSITED	1, 270. 41	856. 64	923. 36	1, 117. 06
FOOD STAMPS DEP.	0. 00	0. 00	0. 00	0. 00
CLOSING CASH	354. 57	345. 64	417. 99	424. 89
CASH OVER/SHORT	51. 93-	6. 31-	0. 42	2. 51
TOTALS	0. 00	0. 00	0. 00	0. 00

	05/05/79	05/06/79	05/07/79	05/08/79
INCOMING CASH				
SALES TAX	23. 70-	33. 84-	35. 07-	36. 38-
BOTTLE DEP. REC.	23. 30-	26. 90-	22. 55-	23. 05-
SALES-GROCERY	994. 46-	1, 237. 76-	1, 308. 07-	1, 152. 64-
OTHER INCOME	0. 00	0. 00	0. 00	0. 00
OPENING CASH	424. 89-	387. 07-	368. 19-	386. 00-
CASH PD. OUT & DEPOS				
CASH PURCHASES	26. 50	40. 45	25. 50	24. 80
COUPONS REC.	0. 15	0. 00	0. 30	0. 00
MISCELL. EXP.	0. 00	0. 00	0. 00	0. 00
CASH DEPOSITED	1, 061. 49	1, 274. 78	1, 322. 80	1, 242. 51
FOOD STAMPS DEP.	0. 00	0. 00	0. 00	0. 00
CLOSING CASH	387. 07	368. 19	386. 00	336. 07
CASH OVER/SHORT	8. 86-	2. 15	0. 72-	5. 31-
TOTALS	0. 00	0. 00	0. 00	0. 00

ACCOUNT NUMBER	TYPE	ACCOUNT NAME	PAGE 1 BALANCE
1010	ASSETS	CASH ON HAND	533.29
1020	ASSETS	CASH ON DEPOSIT	15,034.05
1110	ASSETS	ACCOUNTS RECEIVABLE	2,465.70
1120	ASSETS	COUPONS RECEIVABLE	53.18
1130	ASSETS	EMPLOYEE ADVANCES	574.50
1150	ASSETS	INVENTORY	17,347.61
1210	ASSETS	FURNITURE AND FIXTURES	0.00
1220	ASSETS	MACHINERY AND EQUIPMENT	58,104.12
1250	ASSETS	ACCUMULATED DEPRECIATION	3,836.48-
1400	ASSETS	DEPOSITS	7,466.58
1410	ASSETS	FRANCHISE FEES	5,500.00
1420	ASSETS	PREPAID RENT	1,500.00
1430	ASSETS	PREPAID INTEREST	11,826.70
1440	ASSETS	PREPAID INSURANCE	0.00
2010	LIABILITIES	ACCOUNTS PAYABLE	8,688.75-
2030	LIABILITIES	SALES TAX PAYABLE	1,576.01-
2040	LIABILITIES	FICA PAYABLE	131.22-
2050	LIABILITIES	WITHHOLDING TAX PAYABLE	194.83-
2110	LIABILITIES	NOTES PAYABLE-FOOD	14,426.99-
2120	LIABILITIES	NOTES PAYABLE-EQUIP.	52,547.82-
3010	CAPITAL	CAPITAL STOCK	24,500.00-
3050	CAPITAL	RETAINED EARNINGS	14,503.63-
4011	INCOME	SALES-GROCERY	170,040.02-
4901	EXPENSES	COST OF SALES	118,711.68
5521	EXPENSES	SALARIES AND WAGES	14,992.95
5531	EXPENSES	FRANCHISE FEES	7,047.74
5541	EXPENSES	LAUNDRY AND UNIFORMS	25.40
5551	EXPENSES	CASH OVER/SHORT	47.21-
5561	EXPENSES	RENT	7,500.00
5571	EXPENSES	UTILITIES	5,358.09
5581	EXPENSES	TELEPHONE	214.97
5591	EXPENSES	GARBAGE SERVICE	127.00
5601	EXPENSES	REPAIRS AND MAINTENANCE	374.06
5611	EXPENSES	PAYROLL TAXES	1,429.90
5621	EXPENSES	OTHER TAXES	0.00
5631	EXPENSES	SUPPLIES	769.83
5641	EXPENSES	INTEREST EXPENSE	1,804.66
5651	EXPENSES	INSURANCE	1,158.86
5661	EXPENSES	TRAVEL	0.00
5671	EXPENSES	CONTRACT LABOR	0.00
5681	EXPENSES	AUTO EXPENSE	0.00
5691	EXPENSES	ADVERTISING	0.00
5701	EXPENSES	LEGAL AND PROFESSIONAL	80.00
5711	EXPENSES	POSTAGE AND OFFICE SUPPLIES	3.16
5721	EXPENSES	LICENSES AND FEES	0.00
5731	EXPENSES	MACHINERY AND EQUIP. RENTAL	15.84
5741	EXPENSES	HOSPITALIZATION INSURANCE	428.52
5751	EXPENSES	LOSSES ON BAD CHECKS	136.04
5761	EXPENSES	BANK CHARGES	0.00
5771	EXPENSES	SECURITY SERVICE	135.00
5781	EXPENSES	DEPRECIATION	2,397.80
5791	EXPENSES	MISCELLANEOUS EXPENSE	21.50
7011	INCOME	GASOLINE COMMISSIONS	2,486.36-
7021	INCOME	OTHER INCOME	217.35-

```
        TRIAL BALANCE -- COMPANY: CORNER    AS OF 05/31/79

ACCOUNT                       ACCOUNT                              PAGE 2
NUMBER      TYPE              NAME                                 BALANCE
--------------------------------------------------------------------------

  9999      INCOME            INCOME TRANSFER                    10,057.94
                                                                ------------
            TOTAL                                                     0.00
```

Reports Courtesy of BPI Systems, Inc.—Austin, Texas

F. SOME COMPUTER SUPPLY DEALERS

GINNS Office Supplies
GINN Building
Hyattsville, MD 20782   800-638-0255

INMAC
2465 Augustine Drive
Santa Clara, CA 95051   408-737-7777
                        (has regional warehouses & phones)

UARCO Inc.
121 N. Ninth Street
PO Box 948
DeKalb, Illinois 60115   800-435-0713

MOORE BUSINESS CENTER
P.O. Box 20
Wheeling, Illinois 60090   800-323-6230

ADDITIONAL READING

MAGAZINES CONCERNED WITH PERSONAL COMPUTING

MAGAZINE	HARDWARE-SPECIFIC	EXPERIENCE LEVEL	COMMENT
BYTE	No	Intermediate–advanced	Technically oriented
CALL-APPLE	Yes—Apple	All	Apple users group journal
COMPUTE!	No	All	
Creative Computing	No	All	
Datacast	Yes—CP/M	Intermediate–advanced	Business-oriented
Desktop Computing	No	All	Business-oriented
Dr. Dobb's Journal	No	Advanced	Technically oriented
Infoworld	No	All	Weekly newspaper
Interface Age	N0	All	Business-oriented
MICRO	Yes—6502, 6509	All	
Microcomputing	No	All	

MAGAZINES CONCERNED WITH PERSONAL COMPUTING (*continued*)

MAGAZINE	HARDWARE-SPECIFIC	EXPERIENCE LEVEL	COMMENT
Microsystems	Yes—S100 bus	All	Technically oriented
NIBBLE	Yes—Apple	All	
PC	Yes—IBM	All	
Personal Computing	No	All	
Popular Computing	No	All	
Softside	Yes—TRS-80, Atari, Apple	All	Mostly programs
SOFTALK	Yes—Apple		
SOFTALK–PC	Yes—IBM	All	
80-Microcomputing	Yes—TRS-80	All	

A

ACCESS/80, 125–26, 141
Accounting staff in write-ups, 26–29
Accounts payable, 19
    applications for, 114–16
    storage capacities for, 35, 38, 43
Accounts receivable, *see* Billing
Acquisition, 84–89
    financing of, 86–89
Addison-Wesley, 129
Aged accounts receivable trial
    balance, 112
Alpha testing, 103
Alphanumeric, 146
ALU (arithmetic/logical unit), 8, 146
American Accounting Association,
    53
American Institute of Certified Pub-
    lic Accountants (AICPA), 22, 53,
    131
Analog computers, 3, 146
Analytical review procedures, 25
A/P aging report, 115
APL (language), 123
Apple Computers, 77, 126, 139, 143
    Apple II, 72, 141
    Apple III, 72
    DOS and SOS of, 67
    spreadsheet simulator for, 128
    telecommunciations links for, 131
Apple Puget-sound Program Library
    Exchange, 61
APPLECAT, 132
APPLESOFT, 126
Application generators, 64, 126
Applications software, 12
A/R software, 111–14
ASCII EXPRESS, 131
ASCOM, 132
Assemblers, 123
Assembly languages, 146
Association for Computing Ma-
    chinery (ACM), 53
A-STAT, 79, 141
Atari, 132, 139
    Disk Operating System of, 67
Auditing, 139–41

B

Backing up, 71
BASIC, 12, 13, 123, 124, 126
Baud rate, 12, 146
BCD (binary-coded decimal) system,
    11
Bell Laboratories, 68
Beta testing, 103
Billing, 18–19
    applications for, 110–14
    storage capacities for, 35, 37, 42

Binary system, 3, 11, 146
Bits, 11–12, 147
Bookeeping staff, 26–29
Bootstrap, 147
Boston Computer Society, 53, 61
Bricklin, Dan, 128
Budgeting, storage capacities for, 36,
    40, 41
Bugs, 147
Bytes, 9, 11, 147

C

CalcStar, 129
Cash requirements schedule, 115
CBASIC, 123, 124, 126
Cells, 129
Character printers, 72–74
Check authorization report, 115
Check log, 115
Checks-to-Go, 116
Chip, 147
Clerical staff, 26–29
Client history reports, 112
COBOL (Common Business Oriented
    Language), 123, 147
Commodore, 77, 132
    Disk Operating System of, 67
COMMX, 132
Compilers, 124, 147
Compuserve, 131
Computer service bureaus, 20, 118
Comshare, 129
Configurable Business System, 127
Congressional Record, 130
Consultants, 50–57
    evaluation interview checklist for,
    54
    in purchase and maintenance of
    software, 85–86
Contract programmers, 97
Contracts:
    with consultant, 57
    sample, 158–65
    user, 99–101
Core, 147
C.O.R.P., 126
Cost/benefit analysis, 30–31
CPM (Critical Path Method), 142–43
CP/M (Control Program for Micro-
    computers, 67–68, 147
CPU (central processing unit), 7–9,
    147
    8-bit vs. 16-bit, 71–72
CRT (Cathode Ray Terminal), 10, 72,
    147
CRTform, 125, 126
Customized software, 96–98
Custom-written software:
    installation of, 91–92
    programmers for, 96–98

D

Daisy wheel printers, 72–74
Data base management software
    (DBMS), 64, 126
Data definition languages, 127
Data dictionary, 127
Data gathering:
    for reviewing engagements, 25
    for write-up clients, 25–29
Data Processing Managers Associa-
    tion (DPMA), 53
Data query languages, 127
DATALINK, 131
DATASTAR, 125
Debugging, 148
Decision support system (DSS), 129
DESKTOP-PLAN II, 129
DIALOG, 130
Digital computers, development of,
    3
Digital Equipment Corporation
    (DEC), 77
Digital Research, 67–68, 147
Discounters, 84–85
Disk, defined, 148
Documentation, 65–66
Dot-matrix printers, 72–74
Double-strike matrix printers, 73–74
Dow Jones, 21–22
Draft-quality printers, 72–74
Due-date register, 115
"Dumb" terminals, 72
Dun & Bradstreet, 22, 130
Dynamic Microprocessor Associates,
    127, 132

E

Editor, 148
Electrical work, 80-82
"Electronic bulletin board," 131
Electronic data processing (EDP),
    4–5
"Electronic mail," 131
"Electronic spreadsheet," 21
    applications for, 128–29
Enhanced-print matrix printers,
    73–74
Execute, 148

F

Feasibility study, 24–48
    cost/benefit analysis in, 30–31
    system study in, 31–46, 157
    worksheets for, 26, 28, 29, 156
Fees, consultant, 56
File, 148
Financial statements, 25